RARE
COURAGE

One million people crowd outside Buckingham Palace on VE day, May 8, 1945,
to celebrate the end of the war in Europe.

RARE COURAGE

VETERANS OF THE SECOND WORLD WAR REMEMBER

ROD MICKLEBURGH

with

RUDYARD GRIFFITHS

Foreword by

JACK GRANATSTEIN

M&S

Library and Archives Canada Cataloguing in Publication

Mickleburgh, Rod
    Rare courage : veterans of the Second World War
remember / Rod Mickleburgh, Rudyard Griffiths.

ISBN 0-7710-5906-x

1. Veterans – Canada – Biography. 2. Soldiers – Canada – Biography.

3. World War, 1939-1945 – Personal narratives, Canadian. I. Griffiths, Rudyard

II. Title.

D811.A2M52 2005   940.54'8171   C2005-902309-0

We acknowledge the financial support of the Government of Canada through the Book Publishing Industry Development Program and that of the Government of Ontario through the Ontario Media Development Corporation's Ontario Book Initiative. We further acknowledge the support of the Canada Council for the Arts and the Ontario Arts Council for our publishing program.

Unless otherwise noted, all photos courtesy the Dominion Institute and Memory Project veterans.

Typeset in Minion by M&S, Toronto

Printed and bound in Canada

McClelland & Stewart Ltd.
The Canadian Publishers
75 Sherbourne Street
Toronto, Ontario
M5A 2P9
www.mcclelland.com

1 2 3 4 5   09 08 07 06 05

*"The Memory Project has most successfully
brought together veterans and young Canadians
throughout the country.
In the process it has safeguarded not only
many remarkable stories of the veterans,
but also a unique chapter of this country's history."*

– HER MAJESTY, QUEEN ELIZABETH II,
during the 2005 royal visit, Saskatchewan legislature, May 18

This book is dedicated to the veterans who volunteered with the Dominion Institute and have passed away. We honour you. We will remember.

FIRST WORLD WAR
Paul Metivier, Ottawa, Ontario

SECOND WORLD WAR
Len Birchall, Kingston, Ontario • Hubert Carriere, Coteau-du-Lac, Quebec
George Cole, Calgary, Alberta • John Dix, Toronto, Ontario
Sam Doggart, Sutton West, Ontario • Alexander Esdon, Ottawa, Ontario
Ken Fulton, Toronto, Ontario • Strome Galloway, Ottawa, Ontario
James Glendenning, Ajax, Ontario • Donald Gorman, Belleville, Ontario
Bert Halsey, New Westminster, British Columbia • Charles Hann,
Peterborough, Ontario • William Hawkins, Ingersol, Ontario
Walter Hayden, Candle Lake, Saskatchewan • Milton Jowsey,
Copper Cliff, Ontario • Walter Kelly, Burlington, Ontario •
William Kilbourne, Portage la Prairie, Manitoba • Leon Laron,
Burlington, Ontario Sam Lenko, Edmonton, Alberta •
Beth MacIntyre, Penticton, British Columbia • Donald McIntyre,
Surrey, British Columbia • Bill McVean, Newmarket, Ontario •
Herb Miller, Durham, Ontario • Steve Millward, Edmonton, Alberta
Ralph Morris, Oxford, Nova Scotia • Leslie Oulton, Warburg, Alberta
David Pierce, Ottawa, Ontario • Jean "Tony" Poulin, St. Bruno, Quebec
Peter Rekurt, Fort Saskatchewan, Alberta • Bud Roenspies, Olds, Alberta •
Donald Runciman, Belleville, Ontario • Tony Sarson, Burlington, Ontario
Ron Shawcross, Victoria, British Columbia • Maurice Shields, Oakville, Ontario •
Sam Shore, Hamilton, Ontario • Harry Tate, North York, Ontario
J.C. Thomas, Vancouver, British Columbia • Maurice Tudor, Oakville, Ontario
Robert Van Trichtveldt, Vanier, Ontario • Paul-Henri Vezina,
Ste-Foy, Ontario • James Waugh, Dorval, Ontario
Arthur Westlake, Newmarket, Ontario
Manning Wright, Carleton Place, Ontario

KOREAN WAR
Len Badowich, North York, Ontario • Robert Hamilton, Halifax, Nova Scotia
Delbert Jessop, Oshawa, Ontario • Bob Somers, Fenelon Falls, Ontario
Andre Rioux, Quebec City, Quebec • Patrick Ryan, Toronto, Ontario

CONTENTS

Albert Haywood kisses his future wife, Edith, before leaving for overseas service in 1939. Notice that the sign behind them says "GOOD-BYE."

FOREWORD

THE WAR'S IMPACT ON CANADA AND CANADIANS   JACK GRANATSTEIN

The nation that went to war September 1939 was tired and dispirited. Ten years of grinding economic depression had ravaged Canadians, and the gross domestic product (GDP) stood at $5.6 billion, well below its level in 1929. Unemployment remained high, men still rode the rods looking for work, and wages were low. Moreover, there was little enthusiasm for a second world war. Canadians increasingly saw Hitler as a menace, but memories of the terrible casualties of the Great War, the war to end all wars, remained strong. Despite this, the prime minister took Canada into war one week after Britain and France, with the implicit promise that this would not be a total war but a war of "limited liability" for Canada and an explicit guarantee, primarily directed at Quebec, that there would be no conscription for overseas service.

When the war ended six years later, Canada was flush. Its war effort had been huge, its armies stood on German soil, its navy ruled the waves, and its air force was the third largest among the Allies. The nation's GDP had more than doubled, an extraordinary rate of growth in just six years, and Canadians had jobs, money in the bank, and plans for the future. Social security legislation was on the books to protect workers against unemployment and to give a "baby bonus" or family allowance directly to mothers of young children. The Veterans Charter, an impressive package of rehabilitation and training measures, guaranteed that the men and women who had fought in the war would receive everything they deserved. So optimistic were Canadians, so proud of what they had accomplished, that they even re-elected Prime Minister Mackenzie King in the June 1945 election. The ungrateful

British had tossed out their prime minister, Winston Churchill, but wily Willie King kept his job.

Recounting the story this way makes it sound inevitable. It wasn't. First, victory and defeat were separated by a hair's breadth. The Nazi blitzkrieg had rolled over western Europe, crushed France, and driven Britain off the continent. For a year, until Hitler attacked the Soviet Union on June 22, 1941, Canada was Britain's ranking ally in what seemed a hopeless struggle. The U.S.S.R. and the United States, brought into the war by the Pearl Harbor attack December 7, 1941, finally tipped the scales against Hitler and his Axis Powers, but even then it took almost four more years to achieve victory. The limited liability war Mackenzie King had promised Canadians turned into a massive mobilization – 1.1 million Canadians, or 10 per cent of the population, wore uniform – and conscription became the law, though in a peculiarly constrained, Canadian way.

The nation's industrial effort also went flat out, after a very slow start. By late 1942, Canada's factories, many new ones government-owned, were producing billions of dollars' worth of vehicles, aircraft, guns, and ships, and billions more in foods and minerals came from farms and mines. When our Allies couldn't pay, we gave them the goods under the Mutual Aid Program. The economy boomed, and hundreds of thousands of women joined the labour force, building corvettes, manufacturing Lancaster bombers, and producing munitions. It was a social and industrial revolution, and one that changed Canada forever.

Another aspect of that revolution was the foundation of a Canadian social welfare state. If they were to fight the war, Canadians demanded guarantees that economic depression not return with the peace. The government listened. Unemployment insurance came into law in 1940, a Department of National Health and Welfare took shape in 1944, and family allowance cheques first went to mothers in the summer of 1945. This was a start, the beginnings of a more humane nation. Hospital insurance and medicare were still in the future, but the idea of a welfare state had begun to germinate.

At the same time, emboldened by its war effort, Canada toughly bargained its way into the councils of the Allies. The functional principle, an idea fleshed out in Ottawa's Department of External Affairs, said that a country like Canada rightly could claim to be a great power in some areas. Not on the planning of the Allies' grand strategy – large as it was, our contribution paled compared to those of the great powers. But for food and mineral production, for example, or relief aid to ravaged Europe, or air transport, in such areas Canada *was* a great power. Canadian diplomats pushed the case with great vigour, and by 1945, Canada had achieved general recognition as the first among the "middle powers."

None of these extraordinary changes for Canadians were gained without pain and loss, and we must not forget that, without victory, everything would have been lost, including freedom. The Second World War cost Canada 42,000 young men killed and more than 54,000 wounded. Almost 9,000 soldiers, sailors, and airmen were taken prisoner. The wounded and the POWs suffered grievously and some had the rest of their lives blighted by pain and stress, though many achieved great things when they finally could go home.

The dead, however, were gone forever. Who knows what they might have become? Some would have been doctors, and one of those killed might have found the cure for leukemia. One or two might have become prime minister or party leaders. A few might have become corporate tycoons. More could have been scholars or writers. Among those killed in action was Pte. Alton Kjosness of the Saskatoon Light Infantry, who died in a land-mine explosion on the road to Ortona, Italy, on December 15, 1943. His mother had the inscription "Alton was a poet" carved on her son's tombstone in the large Moro River Canadian War Cemetery, where so many of his friends also lie. Sadly, we will never read Alton's poetry, but his sacrifice must not, cannot, be forgotten. Canadians need to remember that Alton and his comrades gave their todays for our tomorrows. Canadians live in freedom sixty years after the end of the Second World War because of them.

Historian JACK GRANATSTEIN has written extensively on wartime Canada's politics, diplomacy, and armed forces. He was the director and CEO of the Canadian War Museum from 1998 to 2000.

Group Captain John Francis Griffiths, D.F.C.

Rudyard Griffiths's grandfather who died in active service on May 9, 1945.

PREFACE

For some Canadian veterans it was the painfulness of their memories, the sudden recollection of moments of pure terror and acute loss. For others it was the sense of wanting to get on with their lives after giving up their youth to the dull routine and personal privation that is the life of every soldier. And there were those who felt that no one cared, that the seminal experiences in their lives were somehow out of step with a society that seemed increasingly indifferent to the commemoration of its proud military heritage. But now, after a long period of collective silence, our veterans, at last, are speaking out about their wartime experiences.

In schools and communities across Canada, veterans are battling advanced age and their fear of public indifference to talk about the part they played in the great victory over Fascism sixty years ago. They do this not to glorify war. Rather, they are rallying to keep alive the sacrifices of comrades they left behind. And, as they will tell you themselves, they do this to pass on to today's youth a sense of the collective duty and purpose that defined for their generation Canada's greatness and its future as a free and democratic nation.

I have had the privilege over the last half-decade to lead an organization that works with fifteen hundred veteran volunteers across Canada. Both men and women, some preternaturally young, others fighting ill heath and advanced age, these veterans have shared their stories first-hand with almost half a million young people. In their words and gestures they have worked the miracle of time travellers, replacing for a generation of young people the celluloid images of our popular culture and the stilted textbook prose with vivid personal recollections of the war and what it meant for Canada and the world.

Rare Courage is a collection of personal stories of the Dominion Institute's veteran volunteer storytellers, each of whom has related for us his

ROBERT "FLASH" CLAYTON

I went into the militia when I was fourteen. It was the Depression and there was nothing else to do. They called us up a week before war broke out and sent us out to guard the Welland Canal because someone had blown it up in the First World War. Then we came back to Toronto. They lined us up and said, "Anybody that wants to join the RCRs [Royal Canadian Regiment], they're going overseas right away." So I joined. I wanted to go overseas. The next thing I knew I was down at Valcartier camp. I enjoyed the army. But while I was down there, the colonel called me in and said, "How old are you?" I said I was twenty-one. And he said, "I've got a letter here from your mom and you're not twenty-one." I was seventeen, and nineteen was the minimum age to go overseas. So I became an instructor. I did that for about ten months. I was a corporal by then, and they came to me and said, "Okay, we got this regiment from Quebec City, the Royal Rifles of Canada. They need NCOs." I said I didn't speak French. And they said, "You don't have to. They have to speak English to get into the regiment." I said okay. We went to Newfoundland

Sgt. Flash Clayton of the Royal Rifles of Canada in Newfoundland, 1940.

Courtesy Flash Clayton

Canadian soldiers guarding the airport in Gander, Newfoundland,
in 1941. Clayton is in the centre.

for nine months, and then we were on our way to Hong Kong. That was in
November of 1941.

As we travelled to Vancouver for embarkation, we picked up 132 men
from different regiments. Some of them had only been in the army three
weeks. I got the job of training them on the ship: how to load the guns,
how to use the Bren guns, and so on. When we arrived in Hong Kong, it
was November 16. Three weeks later, I was still training them. They knew
that the Japanese were likely going to attack, so they moved all the troops
out of the Sham Shui Po barracks in Kowloon where we were staying. But
I was still there with the recruits at about eight o'clock in the morning,
December 7. One of the recruits came rushing in: "Hey, Sarge, come and
look at all the airplanes." And I went out to look and holy Jeez, there they
were. They started to bomb the barracks. We hadn't heard about Pearl
Harbor. They were just flying over us and they were bombing. I ran in and
got two Bren guns and put some men on them. I spread the rest of the

recruits around the barracks and told them to get hidden. There weren't that many casualties. Later that day, we got on the ferry and went over to the island of Hong Kong. Everybody seemed to be taking it in their stride.

I was right where the Japanese landed at Lye Mun, Hong Kong, on December 18. It was at night. All that time we'd been shelled and dive-bombed and mortared from the mainland, right from Kowloon. They'd overrun that in only three days. That first night, they landed about seventy-five hundred, right where the Rajputans were, an Indian regiment. They were about three hundred yards from us, on our flank. We were only one company, C Company, about one hundred and twenty men. The rest of the regiment was spread all over the island. The Rajputani colonel phoned [Maj. Gen. Christopher] Maltby, who was in charge of the island, and said, "We're going out to meet them with the bayonet." The Japanese just about destroyed them. Hell was going on there. Our company commander was Maj. Wells Bishop, a First World War veteran. He kept us steady that night, making sure we did what we were supposed to do. He was really something else. We were in the pillboxes when the Japanese landed. We didn't even know it because there was so much firing going on all the time. Then, a machine gun opened up, and Major Bishop's head went up with a snap and he said, "That's not one of our guns." We went outside and, Christ, they were already on the side of the hill. All the high ground behind us was a big mountain. When the Japanese broke through the Rajputans, that's where they went: to the top of the mountain. So they had the high ground right away.

I can honestly say I wasn't frightened. I was trained and I figured we could hold our own. It was pitch black and Major Bishop was in the middle of the road, just walking up and down. "Okay, don't fire. They don't know where you are. Everybody be quiet and listen." He was fantastic. There was this Jap on the side of the hill and he began talking to us in English. The side of the hill was all bare. Nothing there. He was telling us to surrender, come up to them and they'll treat us good. And Bishop says, "Okay, I just want you to figure out in your mind where this son of a bitch is. And when I fire, you fire." So we fired, a hundred and twenty of us. I don't know whether we hit him or not, but if we didn't, we scared the shit out of him, because we didn't hear any more from him. Things got really, really sticky that night, but we held our own. Then Major Bishop called the colonel and told him: "They have all the high ground, and in the morning, we're dead men if we don't get out of there." He said he wanted their permission to withdraw, which he got.

By then, I'd been hit. All our barracks were underground in the side of the hill and we'd left the flare pistols there. My platoon officer asked me to go down and bring them back. Of course it was a bad place to be. One of the huts was locked and I couldn't get in. We found out later that our cook and another guy were in there. When they came out the next morning, the Japs worked them over all day and bayonetted them that night. On the way back, I passed some Japs at the side of the road. They would strike their grenades on their helmets and when they threw them it looked like sparklers going off. Jack Cronin saw one coming so he hollered at me, "Drop, Flash, drop!" It was completely dark. I couldn't hear anything. The only thing that saved my life was that the grenade went off right between my legs. I was standing on top of it. It blew my equipment off and I spun three times. My gun flew out of my hand along with everything else. I didn't know that I was in shock. When I crawled up the road, my platoon officer said, "Did you get the fire pistols?" I said, "No sir." And he said, "Well, you'll have to go back." I said, "Well, I can't go back. I've been hit. I can't walk." So he fixed me up and took me into the pillbox. I started to sway. I thought I was going to pass out. The medical guy cut my pants off and bound me up and laid me down on the cot. Quite a while after this, Lorne Latimer came in. He said, "Christ, Sarge, can you fix my Tommy gun?" And I said, "How you doing, Lorne?" He said, "I never had a better time in my life." Those were his exact words. Nothing but guts, eh. Then he ran out the door. He got killed about three or four days after that. He ran over and got behind a Vickers machine gun the British had left behind, and the Japs just stitched him. Somebody told me after, "Christ, Flash, he ran a hundred yards. He had to be dead every step of the way."

Not long after that, and this is what saved my life, Lieutenant Scott came in. He didn't know I was there. His gun was jammed. I fixed it up, and away he went. Then the guys went down the road. They were gone.

I figured I was finished. I was waiting for the Japs to find me. I had a hand grenade with me, because I got to be a little bit of a coward there in the pillbox. My first thought was, I'm not going to get much mercy. Just put it under my chin and let it go. I won't feel anything. Then I thought, What a fucking coward's way to die. Hell, I'll wait till they get in here and take some of them with me. Then the steel door of the pillbox opened and I said, "Well, here come these bastards sure as hell." But Lieutenant Scott came in and said, "Jeez, Sarge, I got a way up the road and thought, Where the hell is young Clayton?" He came back all by himself and carried me out of there. He had a lot of guts. I said to him, "I'll never forget this. We'll have a drink on 'er sometime." He carried me up to a British armoured car that was covering our retreat. They took me to a first-aid station. I was hurt quite a bit. On the way down to the hospital, the Japs opened up on the ambulance and blew the windshield out. I got hit again, in the face. Another guy from my platoon was hit again and died. There was a British guy in the front. He had both eyes blown out from the glass. He was blinded, but he survived.

When I got to the hospital, I was still trying to walk, you know. The hospital was right down at the end of the island, a place called Stanley. They took one look at me and said, "You get on a stretcher." And the next thing I knew, the nurse was there. I found out later her name was Mrs. Biggs. I'll never forget the look on her face. I was really boyish and I could see her looking at me as much to say, What the hell is he doing here? She washed me off and gave me a bath, and asked me if I'd like to have a coffee. I said, "No, I'd like, if I could, to have a hot chocolate." And she went and got me the hot chocolate. She was just a great person. She was one of the nurses later raped and killed by the Japanese.

They overran the hospital on Christmas Day. They'd been fighting around it all night. The machine guns were going. Everything was going. But we couldn't hold them back. They came in about five o'clock in the morning, and the slaughter started. They were just killing everybody inside. I was lucky because I was upstairs when they came in. They did most of their slaughtering downstairs. They put the rest of us into two small rooms. We were all crouched in there. Every once in a while, they

Courtesy Flash Clayton

A Canadian officer greets POWs after the Japanese surrender in 1945.

would come in and pick somebody out and take him out and torture him. They did terrible things. Some of them were real sadistic buggers. One Jap who spoke English said they were going to take the rest of the island and they had no one to guard us so we'd all be shot. There was nothing you could do about it. Then, late in the afternoon, they came in and said the fighting was all over.

Eventually we got moved back to Sham Shui Po barracks. After about three or four months, the guys started to die. They got beriberi and malaria and anything else you could think of. No medicine. Nothing to fight the disease with. But I was very fortunate. The Red Cross finally got through with a little bit of stuff, and there was enough there to help save a lot of lives. Four of the guys tried to escape. The Japanese caught them and beheaded them. Then they put us in groups of ten. So if you escaped, the other nine died.

Then in early 1943, they picked five hundred of us, and we went to Yokohama and we worked in the shipyards. We went out to work every day. It was cold as hell. We had no fires, and in the wintertime, there was snow and rain. If you got wet, there was nowhere to dry your clothes. Our biggest killer in Japan was pneumonia. If you got pneumonia, you just died. That's all there was to it. We had to turn out a certain number of men for work. Captain Reid was our medical officer, a Canadian, and he had a hell of a time because he had to send men out to work that he knew couldn't work, but other men were worse. He just had a terrible job. In March 1945, Americans burnt Yokohama right to the ground in one night, with firebombs and incendiaries. There was nothing left. The only thing that saved us was that we happened to be on the edge of town. They just didn't hit where we were, or we would have gone with the rest of them.

Three days later, the Japanese sent us all up to the coal mines, which were a real, real bad place to work. We were working underground, and none of us weighed more than a hundred pounds. It just about finished us. A winter there probably would have wiped us out. One morning, we were going out to work and the Japanese girls that gave us our lanterns were all crying. When we got down into the mine, no one received a slap in the mouth or anything like that. Nobody was bothering us. So we knew something was going on. It was several days before we found out the war was over. And I guess it was about two and a half weeks before the Americans found us. They came over one morning, twelve fighter planes, just after daybreak. We were all out, and Christ, we were crying and waving, and away they went in the distance. We were looking and looking and then they came back, and did a victory roll over the camp. That drove us crazy. They dropped us a little food and some notes saying they were sorry, but they were off an aircraft carrier and only had so much food. Finally, a few days later, some planes came over and dropped, oh you wouldn't believe what they dropped: cigarettes, canned stuff, chocolates.

Courtesy Flash Clayton

Canadian veterans receiving gifts from a senior student class in Yokohama, Japan. Clayton is in the centre.

Just tons of stuff. [Gen. Douglas] MacArthur had told the Japanese, "I want all these prison camps marked so we can find them. And we're going to be dropping them food, and nobody touch that food. It's for the POWs. Leave it alone. You're not getting any of it."

The next thing I knew, we started down for Tokyo. I got on the battleship *Wisconsin*. There were fifty of us. They took all our clothes off us, disinfected us, got us into a shower, and so on. The captain gave each of us a sailor and told them, "Sailor, look at that soldier. If he wants to, he eats twenty-four hours a day. You take him down to the cookhouse and he eats whatever the hell he wants." After that we went to Guam. I was in the hospital there for three weeks, and then they put us on one of the liberty boats. There were also troops going home, and the captain came on the loudspeaker and said, "We've got people here who were prisoners of the Japs for nearly four years. You'll be able to tell who they are by looking at them. And they're going to the head of the line every time we have a meal." That was really something.

We ended up in Victoria, where they kept us in hospital for a while. Then they called me in and said you'll be on your way to Toronto. When I got there, they barricaded off the street and we had a street dance. It was

Christmas Day, 1945. We always had goose at home, and Dad had cooked up a couple of geese. All the time I was away, my mother had put my Christmas boxes under the tree. And then she'd put them in the closet, until I came home. So that day I got my Christmas boxes. She was sure I was going to come home.

The worst part of it was, the guys later started to die again. The majority never saw fifty years old, and they never got a [disability] pension. But when so many of them died, they began to figure out something was wrong with us. Finally, they got that into their thick skulls. I didn't get any pension at all for twenty years. And then, in 1966, I got $50. It was only in 2001 that they announced that every Hong Kong vet would get a 100 per cent pension. But a lot of our widows never got a bloody dime.

"Just as we were turning to leave,
five or six of our destroyers arrived.
And they went in and torpedoed
the *Bismarck* all night.
As many torpedoes as they had."

ALF HURLEY

ALFRED "ALF" HURLEY

I t was the Depression, and my dad couldn't get work but I played a little football, so I was able to get an athletic scholarship at the University of Western Ontario. I took maths and physics. There weren't many of us. My class numbered five in my graduating year, 1939–40. It was through that that I got into the navy and into radar work.

This fellow Boyle came down to Western. He was head of NRC [National Research Council] and he said, "I want to talk to you guys." This was November 1939. I was twenty-three. He said he could get us commissions in the Canadian Navy as sub-lieutenants, providing we went on loan immediately to the British Royal Navy for at least two years. And we said, "Well, what would we be doing?" He said it was a secret, but it would be something along the lines of what we were studying at school. So we joined up. My decision was based on the fact that you probably wouldn't live too long if you were in the air force, and you didn't want to march all over Europe in the army. If you joined the navy, you could see the world.

Alf Hurley, a radar officer in the British Royal Navy, in summer "rig" on the HMS *Sheffield*.

You're young. That was my thinking. They also recruited from U of T, McMaster, Queen's, and so on. They got nineteen people all told.

The Royal Navy had tested out radar in 1937 on one of its cruisers and found it was great. But for some reason they really hadn't done much with it by the time the war started. In the spring of 1939, the navy named thirty ships to be fitted with the one radar set they had developed by then. But there was nobody to take care of the maintenance or introduce radar sets to the navy personnel. The operational people, the captains, and so on knew absolutely nothing about it. It was highly secret. They didn't even know it existed.

We ended up in Portsmouth where the Royal Navy had its signal school operation. We thought we'd be going into some course to learn what this secret work was all about. But no one said anything. There was no course from the navy. We were put on the parade ground. For three weeks, we walked around forming fours and right forming and left forming and all that sort of thing. The commander said we were the worst group he'd ever seen. And I'll tell you, we were bad. But shortly after that, the commander of the signal school said, "Well, now you guys are going to take your course." So they took us to this civilian establishment on the outskirts of Portsmouth. There were boffin scientists there who were designing the radar sets for the Royal Navy. John Rawlinson, the head of the outfit, said, "Okay, this is what you're here for, to take this equipment to the ships." Seaborne radar. It was called RDF then. Radio Direction Finding. Our total course consisted of eight nights in a row, from six to nine o'clock. Radar is relatively simple. All you're doing is sending out a pulse and getting a reflection and bringing it back to a receiver. The circuits and the design are pretty straightforward. So we learned quickly. We were the first officers in the Royal Navy to hear about it. We were really in on the ground floor. We were pioneers. Canadians pioneering for the Royal Navy.

After the eight nights were over, we were appointed to ships that were either fitted with radar or going to install radar. I went to a ship that already had radar. It was a cruiser. The *Sheffield*. I remember going out on the motorboat and looking at this ship. I'd never seen a cruiser in my life before, and I thought she'd be a pretty sharp-looking operation. Well, this ship looked like a tin can, in my opinion. She'd been doing some work over in Norway and she was painted in abstract green and brown. I wasn't received very well. The commanding officer said, "Who are you?" I handed him my appointment, and he said, "Well, we've got a radar set, but we never use it." Bingo. They had some operators there who had been with the ship since 1937. They knew how to operate it, but nobody was using it. I had no idea where I was supposed to go. I just made my own way. You pioneered, you see.

We were sent down to Gibraltar to join Force H. We had the *Ark Royal*, the aircraft carrier, and the *Renown*, seven destroyers, and ourselves. By then the French had capitulated and the Italians were in the war. The question was: How are we going to control the Mediterranean? The Italians had a big navy. But Churchill was adamant that he wouldn't lose control of the convoy through Gibralter to Alexandria. He had an awful time convincing the admiralty that we could control both ends of the Mediterranean, maintain Malta, and run ships through. We arrived August 29, 1940, in the late afternoon. We were on our way to a convoy at 0800 hours the next day. We were the only radar ship in the group. So we worked out that I would report to the guy on the bridge, and the yeoman would put flags on the yardarm and haul them up so the *Ark Royal* could see the signals about the location of the aircraft. We were the fleet radar centre. And soon the operator said, "I got an echo and it's a big one. It looks like there's about nine aircraft, at fifteen thousand feet, ninety miles away." The flags went up to tell the *Ark Royal*, but she didn't put any fighters up. She didn't believe what we were saying was true. And by golly, there were twenty-five bombers that came over. And of course they made for her. Later in the day, another group of bombers came over and, boy, they were up on the bit then. They were asking for information. After we came back to Gibraltar, they sent a group over to find out what it was we had. So radar sold itself.

The *Sheffield* was about ninety-one hundred tonnes and six hundred crew. We had torpedoes, we had sonar, and we had twelve six-inch guns. The ship was longer than a football field and could do about thirty-five

The *Berwick, Newcastle,* and *Manchester* in action against the Italian fleet.
This photo was taken by Hurley from aboard the *Sheffield.*

knots. By then it was in the beautiful bright blue of the Mediterranean, and I thought it was a lovely ship. I was there when the *Sheffield* ran into the *Bismarck.* The *Bismarck* had been fitted and commissioned and christened by Hitler. She went out in May 1941, with the *Prinz Eugen*, a heavy cruiser. They were located in Bergen, but there was lots of fog and we lost them. A day later, they were picked up by two British aircraft cruisers patrolling between Greenland and Iceland. They trailed them all the way down. By this time, the admiralty had pulled together a group to try to sink her. The *Hood* and the *Prince of Wales* arrived on the scene. You know what happened to the *Hood.* [See Glossary.] The *Wales* was pretty damaged too. She did score a couple of hits on the *Bismarck.* But there was no way she could take on the German ships by herself. So the idea was to keep track of her until more ships were collected and pulled together. Well, early in the morning, the *Bismark* made a quick move and got away. She was lost for the better part of the day. No one knew where the heck she was. Then a Catalina flying boat on long-range patrol found her.

We were coming up from Gibraltar. We were to occupy a spot between where the *Bismarck* disappeared and the French port of Brest, which was in German hands. We got into position and, by golly, that's where the

Catalina found her. Admiral Somerville told us to make contact with the *Bismarck* and shadow her. By making contact, we'd give our bombers a really accurate fix. The idea was that the *Ark Royal* torpedo bombers would fly off and attack her. We sighted the *Bismarck*. We made the contact and the *Ark* flew off fifteen aircraft. There was only one small problem. Somehow or other, the *Ark Royal* didn't get the message about us. It's not clear why, but the message was still sitting ready to be coded. I heard the officer on watch say, "Here come the *Ark Royal* bombers." Shortly after that, he said, "My God, they're attacking us!" They didn't know we were shadowing the *Bismarck*, and they made a full-blown attack on us. I guess the visibility was low, and they were coming out of the clouds quickly and they're imagining all sorts of things. They thought any ship they saw was going to be the enemy. They weren't told we were around. Our captain had to evade. He couldn't fire on his own guys. He was a really great seaman. The bombers came in groups of three. He brought the ship around broadside on before they dropped. Then when they dropped their torpedoes, he'd swing around so he was bow on, and the torpedoes would miss. It was quite a thing. All the torpedoes missed us.

The planes went back to the *Ark Royal* and we were told to re-establish contact with the *Bismarck*. The bombers loaded up for another run. I was watching up on the bridge. It was quite remarkable. They made great runs on the *Bismarck*, and we could imagine the torpedoes coming in on them. We got in close to her then. When I say close, I mean probably eight miles away. But you could see her clearly. She was an enormous ship, more than two football fields long. I saw two torpedoes hit, one amidships and the other the stern. Great spouts of water went up. The one that hit the stern somehow jammed her steering mechanisms. Immediately, she turned and made white smoke and then she vanished. Suddenly, *whammo*! Here she comes out of the smoke and she's staring directly at us. Even before she was out of the smoke, she fired a salvo. It fell a little short. She fired a second, and it went over us. The captain was not going to attack the *Bismarck*. He went quickly hard over to port and laid down heavy smoke. We got out of there in a hurry. We had about a dozen people hit from shrapnel. A couple of them died later on. She was firing high-explosive

A merchant navy poster used as a recruitment tool during the Second World War.

Courtesy Grant and June McRae

shells and when one hit the water, the shell fragments went in every direction. We had a lot of holes in the ship. A shell from one of those ships weighed a ton. A ton of steel. When they hit, they just exploded.

Just as we were turning to leave, five or six of our destroyers arrived. And they went in and torpedoed the *Bismarck* all night. As many torpedoes as they had. By morning, she was not in great shape, but she was still fighting. A couple of battleships, the *King George V* and the *Rodney*, arrived. They engaged her, and she engaged them. Pretty soon, they had fired enough shells into her that she was on fire. But she wouldn't give in. You couldn't sink her with gunfire. Then a cruiser, the *Dorsetshire*, came along. She had torpedoes and she ran up and down along each side of the *Bismarck*, and that's what put her under. We didn't see all that. We didn't want to get anywhere near, to get in the way of those shells. But we heard the gunfire. Those shells are booming. It's an unusual kind of sound.

There's no echo. Whomp. Whomp. And these shells go out at quite a rate. And they travel. A battleship's shells could travel twenty miles. So that was the story of the *Bismarck*.

By that time, we'd been in some pretty rough seas, and there was some damage. The *Sheffield* went in for a refit. But I was told to go to Portsmouth, and they asked me to instruct in maintenance at the same place where we had taken our course. So the circle was completed. Then I went to St. John's, Newfoundland, for the Canadian Navy and taught maintenance for the new radar sets that were being fitted on the escort vessels. For the last year of the war, I was at Saint-Hyacinthe, Quebec, training new radar officers.

Why did the Brits use Canadians for the radar training? That's the $64 question. The only thing I know is that there was a big gap in personnel. Maybe they were short of money. It was the only defect I ever saw in the Royal Navy. Altogether, 123 Canadians went over as on-loan officers specifically for that purpose. At one time, seventy-five of the capital ships in the British Navy, that's battleships, carriers, and cruisers, had a Canadian radar officer. That was pretty well the whole big fleet. Three were killed. Real top-flight guys. Many had their ships sunk underneath them. I think there were seven who later received decorations.

"You could do a 180-degree turn,
pull so hard on the stick, and put
so much gravity on your body
that you blacked out."

HAP KENNEDY

I.F. "HAP" KENNEDY

I was only seventeen when war broke out, so I had to wait a year to enlist. It seemed like the thing to do. We didn't like Hitler very much. I'd enjoyed reading Billy Bishop's book [*Winged Warfare*] in high school, and I kind of liked the idea of flying. I took to it like a duck to water. I went overseas right away, in June 1941, and went to an RAF [Royal Air Force] squadron in September. I remember my first operation. It was a low sweep called a rhubarb, essentially ground strafing, flying very low above the trees. It was cross-channel to the Cherbourg Peninsula. When we took off, my heart was a bit in my mouth. I was flying a Whirlwind, a twin-engined fighter. Our opposition were Messerschmitt 109s, and no twin-engined fighter can handle a single-engined fighter. You don't have the same manoeuvrability. So it was exciting, to say the least. At first I was afraid we might run into a Mess 109, but after thirty minutes, I got my courage up, I suppose, and then I was afraid we weren't going to find one. It was over all too quickly.

Hap Kennedy upon enlistment as a pilot in the Royal Canadian Air Force in 1940, after flight training in Western Canada.

After nine months, I asked for a transfer because on one of those rhubarbs, we had a Spitfire escort. I didn't want to have an escort. I wanted to *be* the escort. So I flew Spits until October 1942, when I asked for a posting to Malta. There was a lot going on there. Malta was a key island, halfway between Gibraltar and the Suez Canal. The whole thing was a thorn in [German Field Marshal Erwin] Rommel's side because he had an army in the desert fighting the British Eighth Army, and here was this ruddy island in the Mediterranean, this fortress, that was helping to stop Hitler from getting at Middle East oil. The German planes were patrolling the Mediterranean and sinking British ships. They would come out of Sicily, only sixty-five miles away. They had half a dozen airfields there.

The first time I flew from Malta over to Sicily, I was flying a Spitfire V and I was stooging along with the squadron when a 109 went by my wingtip. I still remember he had a yellow nose and big black cross on each wing. And he shot down the guy beside me, an English guy name of Jack Dawkins. He never said a word, but his aircraft was on fire and he was going down. The 109 flew between us in a dive at a good four hundred miles per hour, made one pass, and escaped. That was a rude awakening. I was never jumped again by a 109.

The first German plane I shot down wasn't as dramatic as some of the later ones. It was an old transport aircraft. But it made me feel just dandy. There's a mixed emotion, though, especially if you kill the pilot. You shoot at him to knock him down. If he bails out, you say, "Well, good luck to you." We never touched them once they're in a parachute. If he didn't bail out, tough bananas. Early on, I got a Junkers 88 bomber and set the engine on fire. I would have let him set the aircraft down on the water. That was my choice. He was violently kicking the rudders, trying to slow the thing down. But my No. 2, who was a young Canadian, went in behind the Junkers and filled it full of lead. He killed them all. I wouldn't have done that. But he was keen as mustard, and who was I to say, Let them survive. I wasn't going to tell him to quit firing. As far as I know, that was the only aircraft he ever shot down. He was a very good pilot, but not as lucky as I was.

Painting by R. W. Bradford, courtesy Hap Kennedy

Kennedy's Spitfire IX of 401 Squadron over Normandy.

I destroyed seven enemy aircraft out of Malta. I got the Distinguished Flying Cross [DFC] there. After eight months, you were usually posted back to Blighty as an instructor, but I still wanted to fly operational. The group captain who ran the Spitfire wing in Sicily liked my spirit and said they had room for me. We were supporting the army in the field. I was fascinated by this, because there wasn't a front yet in France, so this was the place to be. Almost as soon as you got airborne, you were right at the front. You would go over the line and look for German transports and you'd strafe them. And while you were flying there, you stood a pretty good chance of running into some Messerschmitts or Focke-Wulf 190s, an excellent fighter the Huns had in Italy and Sicily in 1943. We had the Spit IX by that time. They were a good match.

But I got a Focke-Wulf 190 with a Spit V. You're not supposed to be able to do it. But I did it with sheer bloody tenacity. We were flying in the

Strait of Messina, and I saw three 190s bombing a British destroyer. I knew they had come from the north and were based very close by in Sicily. So I angled off to the right and thought I'd cut them off. You'd never catch them in the dive, but I knew they were going to angle off north a bit and then turn right. So I went over land, and damned if they didn't. I was down by the toe of Italy, and here were these three Focke-Wulfs crossing in front of me. They thought they were safe. I slid in behind the nearest Focke-Wulf. I hit him a blast and got a damned good strike. Right behind the cockpit. But they were well fortified, and I didn't hurt the engine because he opened the throttle, the black smoke poured out, and they took off. In no time, they were a mile away. But I left the throttle open in the old Spit V, thinking maybe he would throttle back after a while. I think I chased him seventy miles and sure enough, he throttled back. I moved up and I got him. He crashed in a great ball of fire. My CO had told me to come back because he said I'll never catch them. Which was true. Except if he throttled back, which he did. So I nailed him. The CO was a little easier to get along with after that.

Later, we were covering the landing at the beachhead up near Naples. One of the other squadrons got badly shot up by the Americans. So-called friendly fire. They had come right over from the States and had never seen Spitfires before, and they let this squadron have it. Brought down three or four of them. Killed a couple of pilots. After that, we all got the wide black-and-white stripes on the underside of our fighters for Normandy. I got three more 109s in Italy.

I had some close calls. I never got any holes in my aircraft from a German fighter, but three times I got holes from rear gunners in Junkers 88s. They were all good shots. I did get three 88s, but every one of them punched a few holes in me, despite the fact I'd attacked at four hundred miles an hour.

To be a good fighter pilot, there were several things. The first was eyesight. You had to have good eyes to see the Hun before they saw you. That takes experience too. You don't look too quickly. You look and you stare at a bit of sky and you move your eyes in and around. You scan. That's the word we used. The second thing was flying. You had to jump smartly. You had to be bold. And you had to have a bulldog's tenacity. It wasn't easy. Sometimes we fought against very, very good pilots. You had to be strong-willed and you had to abuse yourself and your aircraft. By that I mean, you had to pull as hard as you could on the stick, and if you did that, you could turn tighter than the German aircraft. Mind you, they knew that, so they had their own tactics. You could do a 180-degree turn, pull so hard on the stick and put so much gravity on your body that you blacked out. You'd ease ahead on the stick, when your vision came back. Meanwhile, the German would have pulled up and done a quick flick turn and he'd be coming back at you. You give the aircraft all it will take. You stall. You turn it at the stall. You know what your aircraft will do. They can't stay with you when you're at the stall. You turn more, and you're on their tail. So they try to run away. Then, of course, you shove everything wide open and you catch them.

I followed twelve home once. Twelve 109s and I was alone. We had had a scrap. Our squadron was broken up. I watched them form up and saw them leaving. I thought, Well, it's all over. I might as well follow them. They certainly wouldn't expect me. I dove down to ground level. I had a Spit V at that time, so I couldn't catch them until they throttled back, which they did. Then they moved in tight formation, which you never do in a war zone. But I knew they were going to put on a show for their ground crew. They were flying maybe eight or ten feet away from the next guy. I knew they must be near their airport and sure enough, there up ahead was a big grass field. I moved up behind the twelve 109s. I was almost in formation with them, but two hundred and fifty yards behind, which was when our guns were in range. Usually one guy was a bit slow. We'd call him "Arse-end Charley" and I picked off the last guy. Nobody was looking behind. It was a great opportunity, but one of my cannons jammed and I missed him all to hell. Then I corrected and hit him with a heck of a good clout. He bailed out right over the airport. It was a marvellous feeling. I put the Spit V in full climb, did a quick 180 degrees, and went up to eight thousand feet where there was some cloud. Then I climbed a bit more into sunshine, and I sat there for a few minutes a thousand feet above the clouds, looking to see if any one of them popped up,

Kennedy (left) and Steve Randall on the Krendi airstrip in Malta around 1943.
With 249 Squadron RAF, Kennedy shot down seven enemy aircraft and shared in
the destruction of several more. These confirmed hits were recorded on a scoreboard
on the airfield. He was awarded the Distinguished Flying Cross for his efforts.

but nobody did. So I went home. It's a true story. I didn't get any credit for
the aircraft, though, because I was alone. No witnesses.

I left Italy around Christmastime, in 1943. I had to get my six months
of non-operational flying before they would let me go again, but soon

Courtesy Hap Kennedy

Kennedy (second from the left) and other 249 Squadron pilots
while stationed in Malta, 1942–43.

after D-Day I went to Normandy with 401 Squadron. In a week or so, one
of the flight commanders got shot down, so they gave me a flight again.
Then a couple of weeks later, the CO got shot down, and I took over the
squadron. That was July 3. I only lasted a month. But I got two more

planes, and I got another DFC. It was really the same job in Normandy as in Italy: close support for the army on the ground. But the flak from the ground in France was much better. Much heavier. The Germans started putting flak cars in all their trains and convoys. They had the right equipment to monitor your altitude and speed. If they could get a beeline on you for a minute, they could line you up. You had to keep zigzagging. There weren't many German fighters around, so we started going deep and looking for them.

I was on my second trip the day I got hit. We'd gone way south of Paris, over a town called Dreux. It was well defended and I was getting a bit careless by this stage, slaphappy or something. It was marked on our map: Stay away from Dreux. They'll get you. And I thought, Oh, go to hell. I flew over the top of Dreux and the flak got me. It hit right in front of my feet on the rudder bars and the engine was just another foot or so away. It was badly damaged. A guy flew up beside me and yelled, "Get out, boss. You're on fire!" I went over the side pretty nicely. I pulled the old chute. No problem. It was a beautiful day and I had a good view of the ground. About halfway down, I could make out a German staff car with four soldiers in it, waiting for me to arrive. But there was a very nice west wind blowing and I think I blew over them three times as they tried to cut me off. I landed and went tearing through this wood into a lovely field of wheat. It was up to my waist. I took five or six big leaps, as far as I could run, and then I got down. The Germans came in their open car. They knew I was in the wheat field, but they didn't know where. They started firing off their rifles. A few shots went whistling by, but they were just random shots. They soon took off and I ran into the Resistance not long afterwards.

One guy went on bicycle to Rouen and got me a false passport. My name was Jacques Michel Kattchix, a Belgian farm labourer. I stayed at this farm, looked after by a French girl and her mother. Pretty quickly, the Hun started retreating and I began seeing them in the barnyard. They would stop in for a drink of cider. I would be up in the hay mow, right next to the cider press, so I saw them coming in. I nearly got caught a couple of times. I decided to leave and try to make my own way back. One morning, I heard a jeep coming along and it turned out to be some Americans. I said, "G'day" to them in true Ottawa Valley fashion. And one of them said, "Jeez, you speak good English." They took me to a compound near Caen. There was a high fence around it, and I was there four days. For interrogation! There were about sixty guys there who had been shot down. Mostly Americans, and mostly they had been shot down by 109s. There were a dozen or so of us Canadians. And we'd all been shot down by flak. Not a damn one of us had been shot down by a German aircraft. We had a little snicker on that.

When I got back to England, I was given two weeks' leave and went up north to see my brother in Bomber Command. I got there the day that he had been buried. They hadn't heard back in London that he'd been killed, so it was really a hell of a shock. When I went to see the air marshall, he said, "You should go home. You've had a good crack at it over here, and if I were you, I'd stay home, because the war is winding down."

It was October 1944 when I got home, and I was aware that the big fight was over. All in all, I shot down fourteen aircraft. But I didn't miss flying a great deal. I didn't fly again for forty-four years. I was a country doctor. But after I retired, I took a course to get my flying licence back and, if I may say so, I topped the class.

"None of us black boys felt any desire
to join up. Hitler was a bad guy,
but there were a lot of bad guys in
Canada who wouldn't hire us.
That's the way I saw it."

STANLEY G. GRIZZLE

STANLEY G. GRIZZLE

I was born November 18, 1918, in Toronto. My parents came here from Jamaica the only way any black person could come to Canada in those days, as domestics. My father worked on the trains and my mother worked in Rosedale in some white family's home, making the beds, cooking, and cleaning the toilets. I dropped out of high school to get a job after the bailiff came for our furniture and my dad needed help. Company employers told me: Go down to the railroad, they're hiring your people. That's the way it was. I worked for twenty years as a sleeping-car porter on the trains.

When war was declared, I didn't join up because I was black and therefore the principles of democracy did not apply to me. None of us black boys felt any desire to join up. Hitler was a bad guy, but there were a lot of bad guys in Canada who wouldn't hire us. That's the way I saw it. One time I went into the gymnasium at College Street United Church, and they were rehearsing a play there, and someone was reciting, "Ten little niggers sitting on a fence." Even in a church I was getting mixed

Cpl. Stanley G. Grizzle of the Royal Canadian Medical Corps at Camp Borden, Ontario, 1942.

feelings. So I didn't want to join up. I stuck with the railroad. But I was conscripted [under the National Resources Mobilization Act]. I received a very nice invitation from His Majesty asking me to join the army. I thought about not actually going, but I got to thinking, You'd better go. How are you going to hide? You're like a fly in a glass of milk.

So I went. I reported to Newmarket, just north of Toronto. They had a camp up on the hill there. It was cold, man. I was shivering. But one of the exciting things was that we had a black sergeant major – the highest rank achievable for a black then. He was a career soldier and it made me feel a little better to see someone like that in a higher rank. It showed that things were not totally impossible. We were all conscriptees. There was an overall mood of "I ain't frigging well going." In fact, some guys skipped. They jumped out of the army and disappeared. But most of us just took it. They looked up my work credits and found out that I made beds as a porter. So they put me in the Medical Corps. We looked after the sick bays in the army hospitals. It was okay. We emptied bedpans, made the beds, and if somebody wanted some attention, we'd get the nurse. At that time, all the doctors and the nurses were white.

We went from Newmarket to Camp Borden. That's where I learned to box. And from Camp Borden, we went to Terrace, British Columbia. It was all mountains. We were training: running up and down the mountains, jogging, getting used to taking orders. We were there for a while. I had a two-week leave when I visited my girlfriend in Hamilton, and her uncle, Reverend Holland, married us there. I decided to book a room at a hotel near Union Station [in Toronto] to make it easier to catch the train back to British Columbia. First of all, we went to the Royal York. They wouldn't give me a room. I phoned the Ford Hotel and made a reservation. But when I got there, they said, "Oh, we don't have any rooms for you." Because they could see I was black. So we ended up staying on Manning Avenue at the home of my wife's sister.

Before I left, I made arrangements with a farming couple, Mr. and Mrs. Bedore, out in Terrace. They were delighted to have my wife stay with them on their farm. I'll never forget them. They were the nicest couple. But as soon as we got back to camp, my sergeant said, "I got bad news for

Courtesy Stanley G. Grizzle

Basic training at Camp Borden. From left: Stanley G. Grizzle, Mel Evans,
Sergeant Ball, Russell Grundy, Al Henderson.

you, Stan. We're moving." "Where are we going?" I enquired. And he said,
"Valcartier, Quebec." Oh my God. My poor wife. She was down. I was
down. We just got there and we had to move. So here comes twenty-eight
sleeping cars for all the soldiers. As the train pulls out, someone said to
me, "Where's your wife?" And I said, "She's back at the farmhouse." The
officer heard about it and said they'd never even thought about it, because
they were so busy packing up. "We might have made an arrangement for
you and your wife to have one of the rooms that all the officers had."

We got to Valcartier and my very good friend and schoolmate Mel
Evans, a white guy, said, "Look, Stan, I'm going to go off to Quebec City
and I'm going to make a reservation for the girls." My wife had gone back
to Toronto, and she and Mel's wife were going to travel up together to see
us. They arrived and we were all excited and we went to the Salvation Army

COPY

IN REPLY PLEASE QUOTE

No. ....

DEPARTMENT OF NATIONAL DEFENCE
ARMY

Valcartier Quebec October 9th 1942

District Medical Officer
Military District No.5
322 St-John Street,
QUEBEC, Que.

RE:- Hotel Accommodation for Negro Soldiers

      Enclosed is a copy in duplicate of a communication received from B-91219,Pte. Grizzle,S.H.,concerning an attempt he made to obtain hotel accommodation in Toronto,for himself and his bride while on his wedding trip. At the time he was on furlough under R.O.699.

2.-   It is difficult for this officer Commanding to make comment on Pte.Grizzle's experience and at the same time confine himself to a vocabulary acceptable to Military Correspondence. That any hotel should refuse accommodation to a volunteer in the Canadian Army who is willing to fight and die for his country is beyond my comprehension, and it is a disgraceful state of affairs.

3.-   "We are fighting for Democracy" What a hollow sound this must have to a Canadian Negro who has met with such an experience as has Pte. Grizzle. The treatment received by him smacks of the "Jim Crow Laws" and the Detroit race riots of the "democracy" to the south. Surely we of the Dominion of Canada do not need to be governed by the opinions of neighbours in a matter like this, if that is the basis of such hotel regulations. If it is because Canadian civilians object to having a negro soldier in the same building, I can only express my humiliation at being a member of the same group of people.

4.-   It is strongly felt that the three hotels mentioned should be requested to write an apology to Pte. Grizzle assuring him that in the future such discrimination will not be practiced.

5.-   It might be stated that Pte. Grizzle is an exemplary soldier, exceptionally clean, neat and of fine character.

    For your action, please.

    (Sgd) (R.G.REID)-Lieut-Colonel
    Officer Commanding,
    No.6 Field Ambulance,
    R.C.A.M.C.

NAT. DEF. B.440
2,000 M—4-42 (4322)
H.Q. 1772-39-767

After Grizzle was married, he wanted to book a room for himself and his wife at the Royal York in Toronto. He was told that they "couldn't accommodate coloured people." This is a letter sent by Grizzle's commanding officer in complaint.

where we had accommodation. The woman there said, "Mel, you can stay here, but we don't take coloured people." Whaaaat?!! I went back to the camp and raised hell. My sergeant's wife was working for the Salvation Army in Hamilton and, to make a long story short, that woman got fired. The lady who was head of the Red Cross for Quebec City heard about it and gave us a room in her house. So we stayed there. It was very nice. She was a very kind lady and I wish to death I could remember her name. I guess there's good and bad in all groups.

All this time I was getting used to being in the army, away from my family. That's training enough. Getting away from your old relationships and experiences. It was July 17, 1943, and we went overseas. The day I got on the boat was the day my daughter was born. They had twenty thousand soldiers on that boat. It was the *Queen Elizabeth*, the first big boat. There was a French guy who would bump me every time he came by. And I said, "You do that once more, fella, and you and I are going to have a problem." But they didn't tell me he was a boxing champ from Quebec City. We had a real brawl. That's the way it was in the army. If you got in a fight, they would step back and let you go at it. But I didn't do too badly, because I was using the Henry Armstrong style of fighting. Perpetual motion. The French guy didn't know which way it was coming. Anyway, I gave him a black eye. It was the first time I'd ever boxed a boxer. We got it out of our systems and that was it.

When we got to England, it was decided that our two-hundred-person Field Ambulance Corps was going to be reduced to a one-hundred-person Field Dressing Station, and the rest of us were going to be scattered around to new units. When they got rid of the old unit, they got rid of all the blacks. There were three or four of us. They also got rid of the Jews, except one. It was unbelievable. I looked back at the new unit. They were all white. So I go from the Field Ambulance Corps, with two hundred personnel, to a casualty clearing station. Then they were looking around to put us in positions. They posted on the board: Grizzle will be on honey-bucket duty. There were a lot of jobs, but they put me on honey-bucket duty because I had refused to be a batman. A batman cleans an officer's shoes and shines his uniform buttons. Well, being so fed up with this racism, I refused. People didn't understand. I don't blame the officers for going down that road because when they saw a black person in civic life, he was a porter or she was a housemaid. So it was a natural thought, you know: "Where's that black boy? He'd be a good batman." I was grateful I had the commanding officer I did, Colonel Gossage. He asked why I was upset and I said, "Because the principles we are fighting for don't apply to me." He said, "You're pretty angry. You better go back to your tent and cool down." I was really mad. I said that I wasn't asking for any special job, but I just wanted to be rotated like everyone else, that I was on honey-bucket duty three or four weeks in a row. He said it should only be one week and they would put me in the quartermaster's stores. I didn't argue because everybody wanted to be in the quartermaster's stores. It was a good job. I learned to drive a jeep. So I was happy, and the guys were all wondering, How the hell did you do that? But that was fine. I also got promoted to lance corporal and later to corporal with two stripes on my uniform arm.

We went over to France thirty days after D-Day. We had to get ashore on this kind of pontoon because the beaches weren't any good for landing. And as we got off the pontoon, so help me, the guy beside me disappears. I was just looking at the guy, and then he was gone. I'll never forget it. I didn't know his name. He just went down, down in the water, and he never came up. He was right next to me.

We got to Europe, and it was something. Every once in a while, you had to fall on the ground, face down, stretched out. A lot of people had nervous breakdowns. Nurses, doctors, privates, sergeants. Many were shipped back to England. They were broken down. We were at the battle of Caen. That's a big city, and man, when we got there, I couldn't believe my eyes. The buildings were nothing but rubble, and you could hear people crying and animals howling. So many people died. War is a terrible thing. We've got to find another answer.

We were often close to the battlefields. We were the first medical attention that an injured soldier would get, so we were virtually up front. And they had to have somebody look after supplies, pick up medicine, pick up the mail, pick up the food, pick up the clothing, pick up the

The medal of the
Order of Canada,
awarded to Grizzle.

bedsheets. We were kept busy. Once in a while, a big batch of injured would come in. They would say, "Grizzle, we need you in the orderly room." It got crowded in there. I saw lots of people die. We had a morgue right next to us. People were lying in bed and dying all around me. Young Canadians. I saw several guys on stretchers I went to school with. I just took it in my stride. I was young. It didn't affect me like it affected some. I guess I had strong nerves. But when I came back home, my mom said that every time there was a bump, I'd jump.

We came under fire many times. I remember one incident. I was standing there talking to this fellow and all of a sudden we heard planes coming. We dropped to the ground, face down. I looked up and saw the cab of the vehicle in front of us was blown off. As was the head of my buddy. I knew the guy. That's the worst thing that I saw. Of course I was frightened. I was young and stupid, but I never felt that I would rather be out there fighting. It was just not my nature, not my style. When I beat up a guy at school who called me "nigger," I felt badly. I tried to box in the army, but I didn't take to that very well either. I never felt that I had to fight. Not at all.

500M-10-44 (5754-5) (ENG.)
H.Q. 1064-81-3

DEPARTMENT OF NATIONAL DEFENCE
NAVY ══════ ARMY ══════ AIR FORCE
STATEMENT OF WAR SERVICE GRATUITY

NAME Stanley George Sinclair GRIZZLE
(CHRISTIAN NAMES)   (SURNAME)

ADDRESS 312 Borden St.,
Toronto, Ont.

REGISTER NO. 464467
FILE NO. / DATE 26-2-46
SERVICE NO. B 91929
FINAL RANK OR RATING Cpl
DATE OF DISCHARGE 12-2-46

DATE OF TERMINATION OF OVERSEAS SERVICE 27-12-45

			$	¢
A. TOTAL QUALIFYING SERVICE	NO. OF DAYS 1359/30 EQUAL TO $45 COMPLETE PERIODS AT $7.50		337.50	
B. QUALIFYING OVERSEAS SERVICE	No OF DAYS 893 LESS INELIGIBLE DAYS, EQUAL TO DAYS @ 25c. PER DAY		223.25	
	SEE PAR. 2 OVERLEAF FOR EXPLANATION			
		SUB TOTAL	560.75	

C. SUPPLEMENT FOR OVERSEAS SERVICE
DAILY RATES AT DISCHARGE
PAY $ 1.70
SUBSISTENCE OR LODGING AND PROVISION ALLOWANCE $ 1.25
ADDITIONAL PAY $
$
$
DEPENDENTS' ALLOWANCE 1/30 OF $ 51.12 $ 1.70
TOTAL $ 4.65 X7 = $ 32.55
NO. OF DAYS 893/183 X $ 32.55   158.84

D. WAR SERVICE GRATUITY		719.59

E. DEDUCTIONS OVERPAYMENT OF PAY AND ALLOWANCES $
DEPENDENT'S ALLOWANCE AND ASSIGNED PAY $
OTHER DEDUCTIONS VICTORY BONDS $ 101.09   101.09

F. AMOUNT PAYABLE
(THIS AMOUNT IS PAYABLE IN 6 MONTHLY INSTALMENTS OF $ 103.08 EACH)   618.50

THE WAR SERVICE GRANTS ACT, 1944, PROVIDES FOR YOUR RE-ESTABLISHMENT CREDIT IN THE AMOUNT SHOWN IN SUB TOTAL OF A. & B. THIS CREDIT IS AVAILABLE TO YOU IN CERTAIN CIRCUMSTANCES. INQUIRY IN THIS CONNECTION SHOULD BE DIRECTED TO THE DEPARTMENT OF VETERANS' AFFAIRS.

SEE REVERSE SIDE FOR EXPLANATION OF ITEMS A B & C

After his official discharge in February 1946, the Department of National Defence issued Grizzle his War Time Gratuity for $618.50 for 2,252 days of service.

I was in France, England, Scotland, Belgium, Holland, and Germany. The week after we got to Germany, the war ended. We had instructions before we got there. No talking to any German women or men. No conversation. The day the war ended, the quartermaster gave us each a bottle of Scotch. I didn't drink, so I brought it home and gave it to my dad. I got back to Canada in 1946. I saw my daughter for the first time. She's now a professor in California. But you know what? We were never close. You know the reason? My daughter slept with her mother every night for three years. Then Daddy came home. You can imagine that it was a bit of a shock for a kid. So she and I have never been close, but much loved.

When I look back at the war, I thank God for the experience. It matured me. Because of my army-life experiences, I became a strong advocate of non-violent direct action in the settling of human differences. I was a chairman of the Toronto chapter of the Martin Luther King Fund, the only chapter in Canada raising funds for Dr. King's American struggle. In 1983, Prime Minister Trudeau appointed me judge, Court of Canadian Citizenship – the first African-Canadian to serve in this position.

"Before the war,
women could be housewives,
nurses, and teachers,
but little else.
The war changed all that."

YVONNE JUKES

YVONNE JUKES

I was taking a business course when the war broke out. The air force started recruiting women in 1942, and that's when I joined up. I was twenty-two. We were called WDs (Women's Division). Of course, in those days, women were not allowed in aircrew. The trades women were acceptable in were cooking, medical, clerical, motor transport, parachute packing, etc. However, in England, in the later part of the war, women were assigned to ack-ack guns and did a superb job at shooting down buzz bombs.

After basic training in Toronto, I was posted to Halifax, Nova Scotia, where for two years I worked alongside a group captain who was responsible for overseeing the building of radar stations up the coast. I kept applying to go overseas, but my boss refused to allow my transfer. When he was away on leave, an opportunity presented itself. Another girl failed her medical, and the warrant officer in charge of postings arranged for me to go on home leave and sail before my boss got back.

We sailed for the U.K. on a beautiful Dutch luxury liner called the *New Amsterdam*, which had been turned into a troop ship. There were

Yvonne Jukes at Westminster Abbey, London, on a day off from the Royal Canadian Air Force Women's Division in March 1945.

Jukes's RCAF identity card with vital statistics, photo, and fingerprint, which was used to come and go on RCAF bases.

seventeen of us in a cabin made for four. We were sleeping in triple-decker bunks. There were so many people on board that it was impossible to feed a person more than two meals a day. If you went for breakfast at six, you had dinner at eight, and nothing in between. The day before we reached the U.K., we were attacked. We assumed it was aircraft, but we remained below deck. Otherwise, the trip was uneventful.

When we disembarked in Scotland, there were volunteers on the jetty handing out cups of tea (you know how the British are with their tea). This was probably the worst cup of tea I had ever had – it had canned milk and saccharine in it.

I was posted to Yorkshire. By this time the Royal Air Force (RAF) had turned over about fifteen stations to the Canadian Air Force. These fifteen stations were to form Number 6 Bomber Group. Ten thousand young Canadians flew from 6 Group, and out of these, fifty-seven hundred didn't get back from the raids. I was posted to Group Headquarters, which was based in an old castle. I worked in the intelligence section. When the bombs were released from the aircraft, photographs were taken of the targets. The intelligence section did the preliminary sorting and assessing of the pictures before they were sent to Bomber Command Headquarters.

Women's Division members put on a concert at Halifax Radio Station
for a recruiting drive program in which Jukes (back row, far left)
acted as announcer and master of ceremonies, 1943.

Being at headquarters, we didn't have much contact with the crews.
Occasionally, when we had a stand down (which meant no flying that
day), we would meet our aircrew friends. We used to go down to the river
and rent canoes. They had a sign, "Canoes Rented to Canadians Only." We
would pile into the canoes and have races. I remember these poor old men
fishing along the banks, who were astounded to see seven or eight canoes
filled with wild Canadians, war whooping and shouting, "I'll swap you my
squaw for a plug of tobacco!" After the races, we adjourned to the local
pub. Some of these kids didn't make it back from the bomb raids, but we

weren't given the luxury of time to mourn. Work, work, work. That was the way to get back at the enemy.

We saw so many extraordinary acts of courage by young people. I'll never forget seeing this damaged aircraft coming back from a raid, when all of a sudden it blew up. I saw a little speck shoot up in the air and one parachute opened. Two days later, the lone survivor, a young Canadian man of seventeen and a half – he had lied about his age to get into the army – came into headquarters. He told me that he was here to see the air commodore, who wanted him to go back to flying again. He said, "I'm not afraid to go, but nobody wants to crew with me. This is my third complete wipeout." He was a tail gunner and he had survived three crashes. I couldn't believe that he wasn't afraid to go back to flying. I told him to tell them to go to hell, that he had done more than his share. Unfortunately I don't know what happened to him after that.

On another occasion, I was approached by the adjutant and asked if I would do them a favour. This was unusual, I was usually *ordered* to do something. They wanted me to talk to this young WAAF [Women's Auxiliary Air Force] and convince her to go out on the parade square to receive a medal for bravery, because she had refused to go. I asked what she had done, and they told me she had been driving a motor transport when she saw one of our damaged bombers crash on the way back from a raid. She drove across the field to the aircraft, which was on fire and had ammunition going off. Despite this, the young lady managed to pull out all the unconscious aircrew, including the pilot who weighed over two hundred pounds. She was a tiny little girl, barely five feet, and weighed about ninety-eight pounds. It's unbelievable that she was able to save so many lives. It's also unbelievable that she was too shy to go out and receive her medal. I was able to convince her to accept the honour that she had duly earned.

I wouldn't say I found my job interesting. In some ways, it was rather horrifying. I was standing outside one night, just as the sun was going down, the sky was red, and everywhere I looked, wingtip to wingtip, were planes. It must have been a thousand-bomber raid. Every station had all their bombers up. The whole of the earth was shaking. And I remember standing there, thinking how absolutely horrific this was, that all those bombs were going to rain down on women and children. Although what I saw in the pictures were railway yards, factories, and submarine pens, it was becoming obvious that there would be civilian casualties, as there certainly were in England after the German bomber raids. By this time I had been in a couple of raids myself.

Once, we had some girls from London with us at a time the buzz bombs had started. This was probably February or March 1945. The war was close to being over. I put one of them up in my little room. She fell asleep and I pulled my cot under the window. Of course, there were no air raids then. Everything was quiet after D-Day. I was kneeling in my cot, looking out the window. There was a huge moon and all of a sudden, a black shadow swept between the buildings and all the glass above my head was shot out. I had glass all over me and there was a whole row of bullet holes just above my head. Then the air-raid sirens went, and I crawled on my hands and knees across the room and pulled this girl out of bed and told her to stay there on the floor. We couldn't go to the air-raid shelters because they were full of water from a flood, so we just lay on the floor. What happened was that we had an aircraft coming back from a raid, and some German fighters came in on the tail so they weren't picked up by our radar. They raided about ten of our stations. There was only one casualty. A WAAF from the transport was killed by a bullet through the throat. This raid was a last-ditch stand. The Free French who had a station close to us lost five aircraft.

I was also in an air raid while I was going to the south of England for Christmas in 1944. I had been invited, along with two of my Canadian aircrew friends, to spend Christmas with an English family. I was not supposed to travel more than twenty miles from camp, and Leeds was out of bounds. It had a big red-light district, and there had been a problem with a Canadian airman who got into a fight because he was talking to somebody's girlfriend. They beat him up and threw him off a bridge. Unfortunately, he hit his head on the way down and drowned. So, Leeds was out of bounds. I took the train to the nearest town and went into the ladies room and changed into civilian clothes. That was something of a

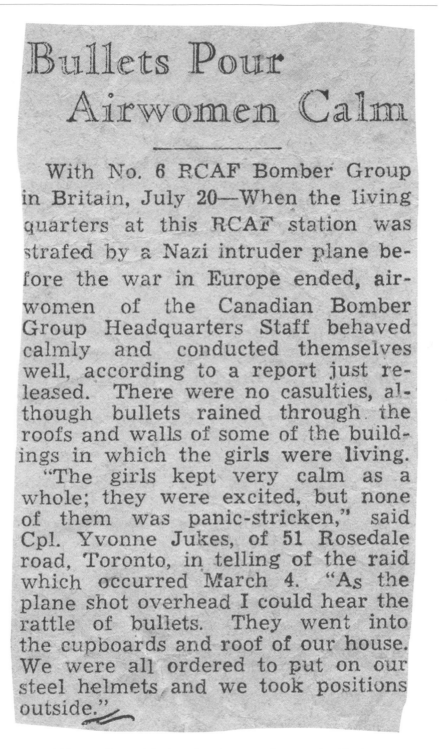

Bullets Pour Airwomen Calm

With No. 6 RCAF Bomber Group in Britain, July 20—When the living quarters at this RCAF station was strafed by a Nazi intruder plane before the war in Europe ended, airwomen of the Canadian Bomber Group Headquarters Staff behaved calmly and conducted themselves well, according to a report just released. There were no casulties, although bullets rained through the roofs and walls of some of the buildings in which the girls were living.

"The girls kept very calm as a whole; they were excited, but none of them was panic-stricken," said Cpl. Yvonne Jukes, of 51 Rosedale road, Toronto, in telling of the raid which occurred March 4. "As the plane shot overhead I could hear the rattle of bullets. They went into the cupboards and roof of our house. We were all ordered to put on our steel helmets and we took positions outside."

A *Toronto Star* article describes the air raid at RCAF Dishforth, Yorkshire, near the end of the war, 1945.

Courtesy Grant and June McRae

Courtesy Grant and June McRae

Second World War
recruitment posters
to encourage
women to join
the war effort.

no-no, and then I had to stay in Leeds overnight to catch the train south. I was at this tiny hotel and a little old lady, as I thought of her then – she must have been sixty – threw open my door and said, "Don't be alarmed, dearie. It's just the Jerrys." I was ashen, my teeth chattering, but I managed to blurt out, "Who the hell else would you be expecting?" They were bombing Leeds. It seems so ridiculous. It's a stupid thing, but when you are young, you think you're immortal. I wasn't afraid of being killed, but what I really thought was, My God, am I ever going to be in trouble if I get injured. I'm in civilian clothes, thirty miles from camp, and in a city that is out of bounds.

Our host in Redford at Christmas was an Anglican clergyman and his wife. We went to Christmas service in his church and afterwards went to an orphanage. We dressed up as Santa Claus and two elves and were handing out recycled gifts to the children whose parents had been killed in raids. As we were handing out the presents, the air-raid sirens went off. The Germans had sent us a Christmas present as well – wave after wave of buzz bombs. Although, I suppose you could say that we were lucky to have had no casualties at the orphanage. We spent the remainder of the afternoon comforting the children.

While I was on leave in London, the war ended, but I couldn't celebrate it there. We had to rush back by train to our headquarters to help in the repatriation of prisoners of war. We didn't waste any time. Our squadrons flew out to Germany the day after VE day to pick up the Canadian prisoners. It was a great feeling of relief that we were not going to lose any more of our young friends. We had high hopes that those still listed as missing might turn up. Some did, but we did get bad news about the others. After that, I spent five months in Torquay, Devon, repatriating aircrews. Finally, there were just a few of us left and it was my turn.

The conditions weren't much better going home on that troop ship than on our initial voyage, except I suppose we weren't being pursued by submarines or aircrafts. I was relieved about going home, but I was also apprehensive about the future. We lost so many friends. Three of my friends went down on the British battleship *Hood*. Our navy friend Johnny Stubbs was commanding a navy destroyer that went down off the coast of

France. He was seen to come up on the shore by some of his sailors and was murdered by the Germans. Two of my air-force friends from Victoria were listed as missing and have no known graves. One other was shot down and evaded the Germans for six months in a Belgian town where he organized an underground movement. He was betrayed and ended up in Bergen-Belsen concentration camp where he later died.

So when the war ended, you came back to a whole different life. My girlfriends had got married and moved away, and all my other friends were scattered. I had to start over again, build a new life. But I could not have stayed home and not have participated in the war. Although there were many times that were stressful and painful, I was proud to have served. Before the war, women could be housewives, nurses, and teachers, but little else. The war changed all that. It altered the whole structure of the workforce for women. As soon as the war ended, women were demobilized from the armed forces, and married women were expected to go back to their household chores. After having been part of the war, women grew more independent and asserted their rights. Now women participate in government, are in the armed forces, and are holding down jobs once thought the domain of men alone.

I celebrate all veterans who have a right to be proud of the part they played in defeating the greatest evil the world has ever known.

"I was flying along, minding my own business, when there was a loud bang. Suddenly the bottom of the cockpit had sunshine coming through where there should not have been."

DUKE WARREN

DOUGLAS "DUKE" WARREN

My nickname is Duke. Nobody calls me Doug. My brother, Bruce, and I were identical twins. Our grade-school teacher said we were duplicates, so the boys started calling us Dupes. That wasn't too flattering, so we just adopted Duke and both of us had that same nickname for the rest of our lives. My father was a farmer in Alberta. When war broke out, he was counting on us to help him out on the farm. But when we were five, [Charles] Lindbergh flew the Atlantic and even at that age we got the idea that we were going to fly airplanes. And so we did. Later, after the first flight of a Spitfire in 1936, we thought, God, if we could ever fly an airplane like that. Basically, my brother and I made all our decisions together. We were very close and we long had a reputation of one of us starting a sentence and the other one finishing it. That's what happens with twins.

We signed up together for the air force in 1941, and from the beginning it was everything we wanted to do. When we graduated, Bruce was

A photo in the "132 Norwegian Wing" report shows pilot Duke Warren of the Royal Canadian Air Force regarding the piece of German anti-aircraft shell that could have killed him and the small tin box that helped to save his life. September 17, 1944.

Douglas and Bruce Warren, identical twins both serving as RCAF pilots
and both with the nickname "Duke," 1944.

one slot ahead of me. He was in the first eight. I was number nine. Only
the first eight got commissioned. So we said we've got to do something
about this, and we did. We went up to Calgary on our leave and eventually
got to see the group captain. Sure enough, I was commissioned too, and I
had the same seniority as my twin.

We got to England and ended up in the same squadron. For the first
month, we flew together all the time on operations. That was good. You
have to understand how fighter pilots operate. You have to fly parallel. A
single aircraft is just like a sitting duck. You need two aircraft, or at least

two, to do some cross-over. And when we were flying together, we had complete confidence that we were going to keep an eye out for each other.

Our first big operation was the Dieppe raid, August 19, 1942. We knew the night before there was going to be some operation a bit bigger than normal because so many squadrons were stacking into the south coast of England. Every aerodrome that could take an aircraft had a Spitfire sitting on it. But we didn't realize the magnitude of it. We were locked down that night like prisoners. Then we were briefed that there was going to be a raid on Dieppe. They called it a raid, but it was really a madhouse in the air, a mad scramble of airplanes going in all directions. There were so many Spitfires, the Germans could fire at almost any airplane and it would be a Spitfire, whereas we had to make sure, when we fired, that it was a German fighter and not a Spitfire. We had three thousand sorties. The Germans launched almost a thousand. And it was concentrated in a very local area, like over Vancouver harbour, say. There were dogfights all around. We thought we'd shot down a hundred German fighters, but in actual fact, it was about fifty, and we lost almost a hundred.

My twin was flying No. 3. I was flying right behind him, No. 4. My flight commander had an American as his No. 2. On our second flight that morning, the four of us shot down a German bomber that was bombing Canadian soldiers on the beach. The German crew bailed out and the bomber went into the ocean. It was a Dornier 217. It's hard to say who exactly shot it down because we all attacked it and we all fired and I think we all had strikes. That was the first aircraft I'd shot down. It was the job we were sent to do.

We'd been low enough to see the tanks on the ground. You could see the shells bouncing off them. We could tell there were going to be a lot of casualties when we got back from our second flight. People were just not leaving the beach. The statistics were almost a thousand Canadians killed and two thousand taken prisoner, most of them wounded. By the end of the day, we knew the Canadian Army had taken a terrible beating. We were in the south where they all came back, the ones that did come back. We met them in the pubs and they said that it'd been real hell on the beach that morning. But I was talking to one guy afterwards who said he was crouching by a tank at Dieppe and he looked up and saw a Spitfire coming down. It kept coming down and nobody got out. And he said to himself, I'm glad I'm down here and not up there. It was just training. He did what he did, but he didn't want to do what the fighter pilots did.

We used to go on sweeps and escort bombers. Sometimes you would see German fighters. Sometimes you wouldn't. It may surprise people, but at that particular time in the war, the Spitfires we were flying were hopelessly outclassed by the German Focke-Wulf 190s. They were far superior aircraft. They'd climb up high and they'd dive and shoot down some person who wasn't watching his tail as much as he should be. Then they'd climb right back up again. But if they stayed to dogfight with you, you would get them because you could turn inside them. We were flying Spitfire Vs. When we got the Spit IXs, that saved our lives.

Certainly on my first tour, I was mostly attacked, seldom the attacker. The Germans would get in a position up sun and they'd come down on you and somebody would call and say, Break, turn to starboard or port, whichever was most suitable. And the Germans would try to turn quickly and be able to get enough lead on you to shoot you down. A number of times I'd be turning, and there were flashing lights from their guns going off, and it gave me a certain amount of satisfaction because I would think to myself, He hasn't got enough lead. He's not hitting me. But I knew damn well if I didn't keep pulling wide, he was going to shoot me down. There was no question of that. But the German pilot, and they were good, also knew that if he didn't get out of there, this Spitfire would be shooting at him. So he would dive away.

The time I came closest to being shot down was over the Continent on a mission to bomb Calais. I was flying along, minding my own business, when there was a loud bang. Suddenly the bottom of the cockpit had sunshine coming through where there should not have been. My leg felt as though someone had hit it with a baseball bat. The shell had entered the aircraft and knocked the trim tabs right off the wall into my leg, but they were big and flat and didn't penetrate. The funny thing, which I laugh about now but was very concerned about then, was that I kept smelling smoke. When I landed, I found that a red-hot piece of shrapnel had got into my Mae West and it was smouldering in there. My life was saved by a little tin box. It's like the story of the mother who gives her son a Bible and it ends up stopping a bullet. This was the same thing. This tin box was in my upper left-hand tunic pocket. And the red-hot piece of shrapnel was stopped by this box. A little tin box.

On my second tour, my twin and I were helping to support the Canadian Army as it fought up the coast after D-Day. We seldom saw any German fighters because they were trying to do their best against the bombers in Germany. But we did take part in the Battle of the Ardennes, the Battle of the Bulge. We were bombing and shooting up transports. It must have been hell to be a German soldier because he could hardly move without a Spitfire coming down after him. Or a Typhoon. Another close call I had came from an American Thunderbolt, one of their fighters. The Americans seemed to be wild men at times. He came very close to me. I saw a lot of tracers going by. We were almost over our own lines so it sort of surprised me to find a German there. Then, when I turned inside him, I saw it was this Thunderbolt. I could have shot him down. But I kept turning and sort of waved to him. And as soon as I got a bit in front, he tried to shoot me down again. It upset me. I thought again about shooting him down, but I popped into a cloud and let it go. I don't think he ever knew I was on his side.

My twin and I went right through the war together. The fact that we were identical was never really a problem. But I'm laughing right now about it because I just got this book from England that has us in it, and the photos are mixed up. I'm not displeased because all our life we were mixed up and it brought back a lot of memories to me. I'm going to send the author a note, saying, "Just leave it as it is." For a long time, even when we were overseas, we always wore the same clothes. We even had the same suits. The ground crew couldn't tell us apart. They put our names up on the side of the airplane, because when they'd go in to see the chief mechanic and say something needed to be done to Flying Officer Warren's plane, he would say, "Which one?" And the guy would say, "I don't know. I can't tell them apart."

Later on, we had to go on leave at different times, and that would be

The front cover of the report on the activities of 132 Norwegian Fighter Wing from June 6, 1944, until the end of the war. It was published in Norway but also sold in England. The number of non-Norwegians in the report was extremely limited, but Warren was featured because of his narrow escape.

worrisome. After you've been a fighter pilot for a while and you've seen a lot of people shot down, bailing out and burning up, you tend to be a little concerned. If I was on leave for a week, I would be worried the whole time. "Is my twin making out okay?" We saw each other have close calls. One day I was flying right behind him as No. 2. We were doing fighter-bomber work and we were using eleven-second delay bombs. For some reason, his bomb exploded right underneath him. There was as great a cloud of smoke as you could imagine, and I thought, He's had it. It just flashed through my heart. Then, his Spitfire leapt out on the other side and he limped home. But we were prepared for this kind of thing. Before we went down from the north to where the fighting was really taking place, we had a good talk with each other. And we said, "Look, it's out of our hands. God will keep an eye out for us, but if one of us does get shot down, we've got to understand that this may happen." That was the end of our conversation about it.

My twin was a better man than I was. We shared that bomber at Dieppe, and my twin had a Focke-Wulf 190, and another one. I had a Messerschmitt and then another share. He had two and half official kills,

Douglas Warren at the sixtieth anniversary of the Battle of Dieppe, August 19, 2002.
The Warren twins flew three sorties over Dieppe, and Douglas laid the memorial
wreath in remembrance of the 403 RCAF Squadron casualties.

and I had two. We were taken off operations about the first of March 1945.
We were waiting for a ship to take us back to Canada when suddenly we
got an order to smarten up and report to Buckingham Palace and we
would get a DFC. It was because we did so much fighter-bomber work.
So we said, "Okay, we're off to Buckingham Palace." We lined up right
together because it was done alphabetically. The wing commander called
out, "Wing commander B. Warren." And he marched up, and the King
gave him his medal. Then I marched up with the same last name, and the
King really looked at me, then he looked back at my twin, and he said, "I
don't think I've ever done anything like this before."

My twin was killed April 5, 1951. He was a test pilot on leave to A.V. Roe
and he had an oxygen problem. Somehow, the system wasn't functioning
properly. He just went to sleep and the plane went straight down into the
ground. We were very close and never a day goes by that I don't think
about him. And of course, that's never going to end.

"I came down in a field. It was maybe two o'clock in the morning. I landed in my socks. The speed from the air when I bailed out took my flying boots right off."

GRANT McRAE

GRANT McRAE

I joined up in 1942. I was twenty. I was working as a junior CA. My brother had joined the air force and my mother didn't want me to do the same. I thought of joining the navy. I liked their uniforms. I walked into their office on St. Catherine Street in Montreal. They said they were too busy, so I said to heck with it. On my way back to work, I saw the air-force flag at their recruiting office on Bishop Street. So I went in and said I'd like to join accounting or be an auditor with the air force. And the fellow said, "You look in good shape. What about aircrew?" I didn't have enough guts to say no. I went home and my mother said, "Did you join up today?" "Yep." "That's good," she said. "Navy?" "No, I got in the air force." "Oh," she said. "You're in the accounting department?" "No, aircrew." I don't think she spoke to me for ten days.

Everybody wanted to be a pilot, but I crashed on the first try with the trainer they had. The guy said, "You're dead." And I said, "Well, that's too bad because I really wanted to be a pilot." "No," he said, "you'll be a bomb aimer." So I continued on with my training as a bomb aimer at Initial

Fl./Lt. Grant McRae enlisted in the Royal Canadian Air Force in 1942, and was trained on Lancaster bombers as a bomb aimer.

Training School in Belleville, Ontario. That's where I first met my wife. She was the start of everything and she still is. I graduated as a bomb aimer at St.-Jean, about ninety miles south of Montreal.

We went overseas in May 1943 to a station up in Scotland for more training. One time, we were on a night mission over the North Sea and, about halfway over, our engine caught fire. We were coming down and we would have to land on water. But the skipper didn't know exactly where we were. At about two hundred feet, we broke cloud. There was still smoke coming out of the engine. We prepared to ditch. And I looked out and said, "Jeez, we're over land." And the skipper said, "For Christ's sake, McRae, get the undercarriage down!" It was pitch black and we were over land, but we didn't know where the hell we were. We couldn't go left or right because the engine was on fire. As we were coming down, lights suddenly came on and, believe it or not, we were over a runway. An air-force runway. They had turned the lights on when we landed and then they had turned them off right away. I was one of the first out because I thought we were going to blow up or some damn thing. As we were taxiing in, I asked one of the firefighting guys, "Where are we?" And he said, "You're in Wales." It was a fighter command station. A raid was on. That's why the lights were off. There you go, eh.

McRae corresponded with his wife, June, a WRN serving in the Canadian Forces, over the course of the war, even while he was being kept captive in Europe. These are letters sent through "Prisoner of War Post" from Germany.

They sent me down to Bomber Command because they'd had so many losses. We were posted to 619 Squadron. There were a lot of casualties, and part of my job, when we lost people, was to get all the stuff ready to send home, all their gear and so on. There were so many coming and going. They'd be gone one night and the next night, there'd be two or three new crews. Bomber crews numbered seven. The pilot, navigator, bomb aimer, engineer, wireless operator, and two gunners, the mid-upper gunner and the rear gunner.

Finally, we began ops. You were scared every night. There were lots of things to be concerned about: The ack-ack and the risk of fighters, and of course whether you'd reach the target on time. It was my responsibility, when we got over the site, to direct the pilot. Left, left, right, steady, and then drop the bombs. Some of the trips were fairly long. I'd be lying down in the front of the Lancaster on my stomach, all by myself, looking down the whole time. In the nose, there's perplex glass and that's where the bomb aimer goes. You can see everything. You don't know whether you hit the target, but you have cameras. As soon as the bomb doors are open, the pictures start. When you come back and land, the first thing the ground crew asks you is not "How are you and what the hell was the trip like?" but "Where's the bloody camera?" They take it right away and develop the film. If you're not close to the target, you get hell.

On our tenth trip, the target was the railyards in Stuttgart. It was July 25, 1944. We got coned over the target by their huge searchlights. Being up at the front, with all the perplex, it was just like daylight for me and scary as the deuce. But we dropped our bombs and were on our way home. After about half an hour, the navigator saw a blip coming up on the screen. The skipper altered course forty-five degrees into Germany. But the blip still followed. He came underneath us and the guns started firing. He shot at our starboard engine and it caught fire. Our gunners were firing, but they couldn't see him. Then he went around again and caught the port engine. A few minutes later, we got the order to bail out. There was an escape hatch right beneath me. I think I was the first one out. It happened so fast, you don't have time to think about it. We were told in training to count ten before you pull the chute. I think I got up to two. It opened up.

It was quite a jolt. There I was, sailing in the breeze. As I looked back, the aircraft blew up. I found out later that three of the guys were killed, and four of us survived. We were lucky. Well, not lucky, but fortunate that four of us made it. The average for surviving a crash was one out of seven.

I came down in a field. It was maybe two o'clock in the morning. I landed in my socks. The speed from the air when I bailed out took my flying boots right off. I tried to remember what the guy told us to do if we're ever shot down. First thing, you take off your battledress and put it on inside out. Take off your flying badges and then bury your parachute. The first night I didn't get too far. I travelled a bit on the second night. The third day, I was lying down in the field and a worker kicked me, and I thought, This is it. But he was a foreign worker and he said, "Je retourne dans une demi-heure." Not only did he return in half an hour, he brought me some boots, a bottle of wine, and a loaf of bread. He didn't hang around too long. He would have been shot if he'd been caught. After a couple of days, I got into a boxcar, but it was very slow and it was going the wrong way. So I had to get off.

Maybe the fifth or sixth day, I got up to have a pee, and this dog appeared. A big bloody German shepherd. He started to bark. Two minutes later, the guard came, and he had a rifle. "Hands up!" That's when I knew I'd had it. Actually, he turned out to be a pretty good guy. He took out a little piece of paper and wrote down the figures 194 and left the last digit open. He wanted me to fill out when the war would be over. So I put down 4. As soon as he saw it, he said, "Gut. Gut." He turned me over to the Gestapo. The commander took out the Bible I had in my jacket that my father had given me. He hit me across the face with it and knocked me down. And he was yelling, "Bible! Bible! Bible! You kill people!" I guess he thought here was a guy with a Bible who was dropping bombs. Then they shipped me to an interrogation camp. I was there for about nine days.

I ended up in Stalag Luft III. That's where the Great Escape had taken place, and all the guys were wearing black armbands for the fifty guys who were shot. I was put in a room with ten guys, five bunks. It wasn't bad living. Red Cross food parcels. Well organized. They had a baseball league. They got the equipment from the Red Cross. They had the baseball games

McRae's POW identification card, issued at Stalag Luft III, 1944.

after supper. The Germans used to watch from the guard towers. One time, a guard yelled, "Hey, great hit!" He was from Chicago or something and was in the German army. I'd played a little baseball and one of the guys said they needed somebody at first base.

Phil Marchildon came to the camp after me. I knew who he was. He had been a star pitcher with the Philadelphia Athletics in the major leagues. He was from Penetanguishene, Ontario. I went up to him and said, "You've got to play for our team." He'd been shot down and they'd landed in the water, but he was in pretty good shape. He didn't want to pitch because he might ruin his arm. He played shortstop. The first time, the ball went out to him, he threw it to me and, God, he put a curve on it. It was going left and right and I missed it by about five feet. All the guys on the side were laughing like hell because they didn't know who he was. I told him at the end of the inning, "Phil, just take it easy."

Of course he could bat too. We had a game against the Americans, and that was fun because those guys had a pretty good team. But we had a decent team too. A lot of the guys were from out west. They were good ballplayers. At any rate, Phil got up to hit. He took three bats like the big guys do, and one of their guys looked at me and said, "Where's that guy from? He looks like he's played ball before." And I said, "He's from Canada and he's played ball a little bit." Christ, he gets up at bat and he knocks it out. It went right over the fences and into the woods. I think the Germans are still looking for it. When I told the other guys who he was, that just killed them. They didn't know he was a Canadian. We won the game. So that was quite a lot of fun.

In November, it started to get cold and we got a hockey league going. We got the skates and sticks from the Red Cross. They let us come out at night and hose down the rink. The skates we got were the ones that you put on the bottom of your boots. Phil played too. He didn't skate that well, but he could shoot. He was a super guy.

By the middle of January 1945, the Russians were advancing and we could hear the guns going off. One night around ten o'clock, the Germans came into the rooms and said, "Get ready, because we're leaving the camp in two hours." They said we were going on the road. It was about ten below zero. Colder than hell. There was real panic. Guys were breaking up bed boards and doors to make sleighs. Two guys to a sleigh. We took as much food and clothing as possible. Then we started off on the march. It was scary because we didn't know where the heck we were going. There must have been thousands of us, walking. We stopped in a church one night, and we burned the pews, sacrilegious as hell, to keep warm. Then the camps split up. Some guys went north. We were put into boxcars and they slammed the doors shut. It was terrifying. We didn't know what was going on.

We finally arrived at a camp called Luckenwalde. It was a terrible camp. I think there were one hundred and forty of us to one room. The bunks were four beds high. No Red Cross parcels. Cold. We just lay in the bunks all day, starving. Until April, I guess, when we were liberated by the Russians. A Russian tank came through. The tank commander had two or three guys with him and they had bandages on and everything. They were going on to Berlin. They threw us some rifles and they wanted us to join them. And we said, To hell with that noise. You guys go ahead. Three hours later, more tanks came through. Then the army.

In April 1945, the first Russian tank rolled into Luckenwalde camp.
After negotiations with Moscow, the prisoners of the camp were finally released.
This photo shows the compound of an air force POW camp in Germany.

The war was over in May, but we stayed on in the camp because the Russians wouldn't let us leave. Some American truck drivers came one day with orders from Eisenhower to liberate all British and American personnel. So we got in the back of the trucks, but the Russians, who were supposed to be our Allies, fired over our heads. We had to get off. Some of the guys were practically crying because they'd been there three or four years and this was their first chance to get out. The Russians said the orders had to come from Moscow. They said they didn't know anything about Eisenhower. The trucks went back empty. We had no way out. We wondered if the Russians were going to send us to the salt mines. At last, some Russian troops took us to the Elbe. That's where the dividing line was. We got out of the trucks and walked across a Bailey Bridge built by the American engineers. We were liberated.

"We were lying on our bellies in this
bloody ditch. His face was about
six inches from me, and the ground was
shaking and the tank was coming at us.
I said, 'This looks like it, Tom.'
And he said, 'It sure as hell does.'"

PETER COTTINGHAM

PETER COTTINGHAM

I was born in 1921 in the Swan River Valley toward the north part of Manitoba. I was in Grade Twelve when the Germans overran France and all of Europe. It looked like the end of the world. I didn't even wait to graduate. I just went to Winnipeg to join up. Dunkirk was four days later. [See Operation Dynamo in Glossary.] I trained for about a year and I was going to put my name on a list to go to Hong Kong with the Winnipeg Grenadiers, but a friend put our names in with the Regina Rifles to get to England instead. I was there for a year and I was the only one of two hundred who volunteered that they took into the paratroops.

I'm not too proud of how I got in there. I'd been helping to run people through this commando course at a battle school. It was pretty strenuous. One time, I was in the pub having a rum with a couple of Brit sailors and they said there's a boat down at the docks about to leave for France on a commando raid. I said, "Wow, let's go along." I said I knew all about commando raids. My own guys were on guard at the dock, so we went right on by. I got on the ship and said, "We need rifles, if we're going to go with you

Peter Cottingham at Fort Osborne, Winnipeg, in 1941. Cottingham was Battalion Operations Chief of the 1st Special Services Force.

guys." They said, "Get off this ship." And they locked us up. So that night I was in the brig. No charges. Just keep your mouth shut. The next morning, the brigadier was inspecting the brig and there I was. "Corporal Cottingham, what are you doing here?" And the sergeant major with him said, "This man was found on board a landing craft about to depart for France last night. Sir!" By that time, we knew it was Dieppe. My God! I tried to throw my life away more than a few times. Two weeks later, I was the only guy in the regiment who got picked out of these two hundred for the paratroopers. I guess the brigadier knew the name and thought, Well, this bugger should go.

We went to Fort Benning, Georgia, where they were training the 1st Canadian Paratroop Battalion. Then, some guy from Montana came down and talked seventeen of us into joining this secret outfit that was called the Special Services Force. They would be training at a secret camp in the mountains. That sounded pretty good to me. So we went up there, near Helena, Montana. Shortly after we got there, we found out that we were training for a kind of suicide mission. They were going to drop us into Norway to destroy a heavy-water project. We thought it was suicide because after we blew up the hydro plant, we were supposed to ski over to Sweden. We thought we'd either be taken prisoner or shot. So we did all this training: skiing, mountain climbing, demolitions, the whole bit. Right through the winter. We ended up with three regiments, six hundred guys to a regiment. Half were Canadians. We'd ski up mountain passes and live in unheated boxcars. We had sleeping bags. We were tough guys. It got to be forty, forty-five below, and there were guys from Texas who had never seen snow before. They put us through a lot of stuff, like rappelling down a cliff with a wounded guy on your chest. They weeded us out. When they decided to scrap the Norway mission, there was a big sigh of relief.

The first job we had was to go to the Aleutian Islands [off the southwest tip of Alaska]. The Japanese had taken a couple of those islands and they belonged to the United States. I was battalion operations sergeant, so I was right in the driver's seat. We were first to paddle ashore in the middle of the night, all camouflaged, our faces black. This was Kiska Island. We assumed the Japanese there were going to make another suicide stand like

Cottingham's
Canadian
paratroop wings.

they did on Attu Island. We were prepared to tangle with them. This was going to be our first action and I was excited. Kiska was a long island and mountainous. You could hardly see anything in the fog. But we went right to the top of this mountain and got into a Japanese bunker. We found hot coffee in there. We had a radio operator to call in artillery from the ships offshore. What we heard on his radio at 6 a.m. were shells exploding in their main camp and excited Japanese shouting. So they were still on the island. Later, the U.S. Navy said officially that the Japanese left before we got there. Well, I'm probably one of the few people who heard them. There was bad, bad fog that morning, and we figure they got away on submarines. I think the navy was red-faced and didn't like it to be known that they escaped. The reports that said the Japanese evacuated the island three weeks earlier were a lot of eyewash.

Then everyone was shooting at each other. That was terrible. I was right in the middle of that. We were down in the valley and I heard this machine-gun fire going on all around us. It was the 87th Mountain Infantry. They were shooting at each other. It was so foggy. They were scared. They'd see these heads moving and they'd think it was the Japanese coming. I couldn't believe these guys. I guess the 87th had the shit scared out of them. I saw thirteen bodies brought down the next morning on stretchers. But a documentary I saw the other night said about eighty-two guys were killed that night. By their own people. We were there about a week. There were no Japanese anywhere.

Three months later we were in North Africa. We landed in Casablanca, which looked like Pearl Harbor. The French fleet had been scuppered, and funnels and stacks were sticking out of the water all over the place. We got on the boxcars and rode through the Atlas Mountains to Oran. Then we sailed to Naples. That's when we got into the real war. It was terrible. Terrible. That's where I got wounded. I was very, very fortunate to get wounded there, because the guy who took my place in battalion headquarters, his head rolled down the hill into another guy's foxhole about a week later. It was really rough.

The mountains and the cold and the rain and the shellfire. We were trained for this, but jeepers, I expected something a little more clandestine, you know. We were just used as infantry. I wasn't in the battalion that scaled Mount La Difensa [a famous daredevil exploit of the Special Services Force]. We were backup. Unfortunately, they sent us around the mountain before the place got dark enough. So we were sitting ducks for every German gun in the Liri Valley. They hammered us all night long until they ran out of ammunition. They had to wait for some more trucks to bring them more shells. So I stood up and my foot started hurting. But I never even looked at it. Then, we were going down this trail and someone said, "What happened to your foot?" I said, "I think a rock hit it." "Well," he said, "there's blood coming out of the eyehole of your boot." And I looked down and there was blood squeezing out. A piece of shrapnel had gone right through my foot. I took off my boot, and my foot swelled up, so they had to put me on a stretcher and carry me down the mountain. I was in hospital for thirty-seven days. That wasn't too much fun, but you should have seen the guys stuck in that ward, the stuff that was torn off them. . . . It took a lot of the glamour away.

I got out of the hospital in time to go to the Anzio beachhead landings, seventy-five miles north of Naples. After landing there around February 1, we didn't break out until May 23. And we fought all the way to Rome. Once, we followed these tanks across a little bridge into a hail of fire. It was like going over the top in the First World War. I was right beside my colonel when he got killed there. We hadn't gone fifty yards. I don't know what keeps you going when that happens. It's just that you have to go, you know. It's a hell of a feeling. You can hear these bullets snapping around you. You can't think about it. If you did, you'd quit. It's a lot different from your training, when nobody's shooting at you.

Eventually, we met up with our second front and tried to cut off the Germans escaping out the Liri Valley. That was another battle. We lost about forty-five guys in that one. And I lost another colonel. I think a bullet from a flak wagon got his head. By late afternoon, we ran into five German Tiger tanks. When they came over the railway overpass, we were in a farm building that had two-foot-thick walls. They fired a shell into the tank officer's room and killed him. The tanks had 88 mm guns on them. Their velocity was so great, you couldn't hear the shells coming. They put one right through the room I was in. That was a hell of a thing. All I could see through the grime and dust was the open door. I ran out and we went back into a ditch. Everybody that stood up in the ditch got mowed down by a tank. I was face to face with another guy. We were lying on our bellies in this bloody ditch. His face was about six inches from me, and the ground was shaking and the tank was coming at us. I said, "This looks like it, Tom." And he said, "It sure as hell does." Just then, somebody hit the tank with a bazooka. We could hear the guys in the tank yelling and screaming and the ammunition popping in there. It was something.

Actually, I don't even like to talk about it. When I think of Bush starting a war, I can't believe the idiot. War is a horrible thing. It's a last, last resort. Churchill said, "Jaw, jaw, jaw is better than war, war, war." Mind you, it was a little different when I joined up. The war had been started by Hitler. In occupied Europe, people were up for grabs. Men were up for grabs, women were up for grabs, your bicycle was up, your car. Anything they wanted, they took.

For me, anyhow, that was the worst day. About a week later, we got on some trucks at night and headed down the road to Rome. Our outfit was the first one in. We were the guys who liberated Rome. But I'll tell you, we had six hundred guys in our regiment when we left Anzio, and we had sixty when we got into Rome. Not all dead. A lot wounded and some taken prisoner. Rome was pretty well intact when we entered. Our outfit had to make sure that they didn't bomb all the bridges across the Tiber. It was a big relief to be in Rome. I got a room in the Hotel Excelsior, which was one of their better hotels. That was one of the first times I saw a bidet. At least I knew what it wasn't for! We weren't in Rome that long. We pulled out and

Cottingham in 2000,
at Fort Osborne, Winnipeg,
in the same place he was
photographed in 1941
(see page 65). He is holding
a plaque of the cover from his
book, *Once Upon a Wartime*.

they took us out to bivouac in the garden of the Pope's summer home, the Castel Gandolfo. It was next to a small volcano and it was beautiful. There was a three-mile-wide lake at the bottom and orchards all the way around. The Pope's summer palace was up on the ridge. From there, we left to go train for the landings in southern France.

Those landings were a lot better, but we did lose some people on that bloody Port Cros Island that we should not have lost. That was stupid. One of my best friends was killed trying to attack one of the forts on the island, when we could have just let the bastards starve to death in there. It was a waste of good people. These were the watchdog islands for the big base at Toulon. We had to go in and take out the big guns. We paddled ashore one year to the hour from the time we landed on Kiska. By then, we were more than a little shell-shocked.

The Special Services unit was disbanded in December 1944. They felt the war had advanced beyond the point where they needed us. They could now spearhead with tanks and stuff like that. Some people like to say there wasn't a dry eye when we held our last parade, but I wasn't crying. I'm sure we spent about two hundred days in contact with the enemy. It was awful. But in retrospect, you couldn't pay to do what I did. It was just so fantastic to know the guys I knew. It was a lifetime experience that very few people should have. Once you have it, you can't take it away. I'm glad I experienced it.

After VE day, I was in an officers school in Britain learning how to fight in the jungles of Burma. The army owned me. I was just a bloody volunteer, you know, but once you sign up, they own you. When they dropped the bomb on Hiroshima, I thought, I'm going to live.

"It was exciting. Startling.
The air was filled with bomb
explosions and answering gunfire.
Fear didn't come into it
until afterwards."

BRUCE LITTLE

BRUCE LITTLE

We lived on a farm in Woodrow, Saskatchewan. I left Grade Nine to join the army. It was a great thing for me. I was in England before I was seventeen. I'd only been to Regina before then. I lied about my age. A buddy and I went in. He was a year older than me, but I was tall, as well as young and stupid. We both said we were nineteen. The army would accept anyone as long as they had two of everything: Two eyes, two ears, two legs. I think they knew we were under-age, because they put us in the artillery, where your chances of survival were a hell of a lot better because you're a mile behind everything.

We went over in February 1941. It was damn cold and miserable. I was so seasick for the first three days I was praying for someone to shoot me. I took one look at those waves and that was that. My face was green. One night, there was a thunderous noise and a wall of water shot by our cabin door. I thought we'd been torpedoed. I was sure we were sinking. Two sailors came by. There was a clang, another clang, and then they went by

Bruce Little, a gunner in the 1st Light Anti-Aircraft Regiment, at age nineteen in June 1943. He had already been in the army for three years when this photograph was taken.

Little's electrical class in Barryfield (Kingston), Ontario, before he left
for Korea in 1950. Little is in the bottom row, second from the right.

our door muttering, "Those stupid goddamned soldiers. They look out
the porthole and don't close it properly." The water came through there
just like a firehose.

We ended up in Colchester in light anti-aircraft. One night, there was
an alert from the town. Then there was an imminent alert. We took this to
be the all clear. We got down off the Bofors gun and were about to relax
when eighteen German fighter bombers shot by us just like that. I think
we managed to get six or eight shots away. They came in under five hundred feet, so the radar didn't spot them. If I'd known one of the pilots,
I could have waved to him. That's seeing the enemy up close. We were all

a little upset, because we thought we had been less than professional. Rather than having the guns turned toward them when they came, we were sitting off to an angle. We had the ammunition ready but didn't even have it in the barrel. We would have been better off with a machine gun. Or my .22.

By the time we left to go to Italy, we were all bored to tears, sitting around doing nothing. On the way down, our convoy was attacked in the Mediterranean. We were just past Gibraltar. It was a beautiful evening, a time you'd want to have a girl on your arm. I was up on deck and we got attacked by a bunch of Junkers 88s. Most of us were chased off the deck, so we only saw the planes coming in on the first wave and that was it. But it was exciting. Startling. The air was filled with bomb explosions and answering gunfire. Machine guns, pom-poms, and the sharp crack of ack-ack guns joined in to drive them off. Fear didn't come into it until afterwards, when you were hidden down in the hold and you couldn't do anything. You couldn't shoot back. Pretty frustrating.

We landed in Sicily. The 1st Division went in ahead of us, and they did all the fighting. But it was really interesting. Sicily was extremely dry and extremely poor. We used to sprinkle salt on the roads to attract some moisture so the roads wouldn't be dusty and draw shellfire. The natives would come along and pick up the salt. They were that poor. They would take anything. Then we wound our way up through Italy. It was spectacular going through the mountains. One of the things I remember were these Italian prisoners of war working on the road. Pick-and-shovel work. This was a mountainous road and when it was raining and we'd go by, they'd be standing to one side, maybe a man every truck length, and they would be singing an opera. One guy would be a bass, the next guy would be a tenor, and the next guy would be a soprano or something. It was a memorable experience for me to hear all those beautiful voices. They really didn't want to be in the war in the first place.

I was still with light anti-aircraft. At Ortona, they used us as field artillery, but this was kind of stupid, I thought. They had us up as close to the line as we could get, and our captain was watching with binoculars. He saw some action in the distance at a house and he called down each one of our guns on it. We weren't very accurate. Then he had us fire ten rounds each at the thing, and I'm sure we lifted the paint off it in several places. So the guys from the big field artillery called down one shot, and blew the house all to hell.

The Germans were damn good fighters and well entrenched in Italy. Every battle was a fierce battle. But for us, being in ack-ack [anti-aircraft division], it was not very often that we were in a vulnerable position. The field artillery had to be up closer than we were. But one night, when we were up in the hills about forty miles from Bari, we saw an air raid. That was the only time in that part of the world that I saw one. The Germans sank a bunch of our ships. We couldn't hear anything, but we could see it from a distance, and it was quite a sight. About three or four years ago, the mayor of Bari was raising hell that the ships sunk that night were rotting in his harbour and one of them was filled with poison gas. And guess who's poison gas it was? It was ours. It was only there to retaliate with if the Germans used it, but when you talk about weapons of mass destruction, none of us was without dirty hands.

By then I was a truck driver and not often on the guns. I grew up on a farm and city kids hadn't been drivers. They didn't know anything about mechanics. I was a driver-mechanic, so they eventually sent me to the 7th Anti-Tank Regiment and then I became a member of the RCRS [Royal Canadian Regiment] because the infantry wanted someone with track experience. That was late in 1944. The Germans had flooded a huge section of the land. We had about three feet of water in our sector, and the Americans had what they called a secret weapon. It was the Weasel. It was about the size of a jeep, with tracks and high side walls on it, so it was amphibious. It could go sixty miles an hour on the road and four miles an hour across water. We had two of them assigned to the RCRs. They were the only vehicles that could move in this sector. They'd just designed it, so it was secret. Sitting right behind the driver's seat were three pounds of high explosives and a red button that you pushed and three minutes later, the thing would be all blown to blazes. They said, Push that button and run like hell. Only if the Germans were going to capture you, of course. They thought the technology was something special.

I remember the first time I drove a Weasel. It was really exciting. They were very light and quite responsive. You drove them with two tillers rather than a steering wheel. You put a brake on one track, forward the other, and that was the way you steered. The driver sat up right next to the engine and three people would sit in the back, and that was it. We used them to carry ammunition and bodies and food and virtually everything at that stage of the game. We also carried stretchers on the top. Before this, we didn't have any amphibious vehicles. This thing was actually made for the Arctic, and it had a very light footprint. There was no armour and the metal was very thin. You could drive over most mines without them exploding. The tracks were about seventeen to eighteen inches wide, held together by a core of rubber, and they went the full length of the vehicle. It would do everything. It really worked.

I was on a road one day and the Germans must have caught wind of me. Have you heard of the Moaning Minnies? The six-barrelled mortar the Germans used? They were psychological as much as anything. They were big dumb things that blow up. And they made an eerie sound that just caused the hair to stand right up on the back of your neck. These things started following me down the road. I think I was doing sixty when I looked up and some of our guys had dug a slit trench right in the middle of the road. There were two guys in there facing me. It was too late for me to do anything else. Their heads disappeared down into the trench and I kept going. I didn't want to go down that road for a few days afterwards.

It was frightening to be under fire, but it was also exciting. I guess I was still pretty young, you know. Just eighteen. I really wasn't supposed to be overseas at that age. There were a couple of us underage guys in our outfit, but if we'd complained about our age, they would have sent us home. Then we would have been boy soldiers.

One time we were taking up lunch to this stone house, and I was waiting for our guys to finish, and we were shelled by the Germans. Normal procedure was to put your back against the wall so the roof didn't come down on you. The shell blew the roof in, and when it exploded it couldn't have been any more than ten feet away from me. That was the closest call I ever had. But the captain there, who was a really good friend of mine,

Bruce Little's medals (from left): 1939–45 Star, Italy Star, Defence Medal,
Canadian Volunteer Service Medal with eighteen months overseas bar,
War Medal, Canadian Korean Medal, Canadian Volunteer Service
Medal for Korea, UN Korea Medal with silver cross.

was killed. He had a pair of American gloves with cloth backs and leather laces. He knew I always liked those, and he said to me, "You can take them." He said that as he was dying.

After the shelling, I went to another house nearby and one of the guys asked me what happened. He was eating some chicken and standing in front of a fireplace. And I said, "Well, we've lost the captain." He threw the chicken in the fire and turned around and went away. The next day, when they were about to go into action, he was crying and wouldn't go. The captain was his best friend. And this guy was really a super soldier before that. He just kind of got to where more and more people next to him had gone down the tube, and he couldn't take it any more. You do get a little numb or else you go crazy. In this case, I took the officer back. I think there were four other people that had died that day in our company. We buried them in shallow graves. No fanfare. I wrote out something to say. There was no Governor General there to say a few words. We didn't have any of that.

We were stalemated at that point. The Germans blocked us. We couldn't move. Just about that time, I was called home, so I didn't get to see the finish of it. My father was ill and used some political pressure to get me home. I didn't really want to go, but if I'd said that out loud, I would have been jeered out of the outfit. Because everybody wanted to go home. And so, away I went.

  I don't think I had any vision of what war was like when I joined up. Probably just romantic ideas, which were a long way from reality. But I was still excited by a lot of it. It was an adventure. When I got home, it was nice to be out of it alive. But I was farming. At ten o'clock in the morning, a time when I usually had a bunch of guys around for coffee, here I was out in the middle of the prairie. I felt I was the loneliest guy on earth. So it was a mixed blessing.

"One little mortar fluttered
in and it hit somebody.
Bill Carpenter said,
'Who did that hit?'
And I said, 'Me.'"

GORDON BANNERMAN

GORDON BANNERMAN

I was born in 1921 on a farm in Saskatchewan where my dad homesteaded. I signed up in July 1940. It was a time when there wasn't a ruddy penny anywhere, when you think your dad might have put the last fifteen cents in the house in the Sunday collection plate. I joined the 60th Battery of Royal Canadian Artillery in Aneroid, Saskatchewan, and went overseas November 9, 1941.

We were sent to Italy in 1943. Our convoy got torpedoed on the way over after we went through Gibraltar. Our ship didn't get hit, but one with a lot of nurses on board went down. The girls rode the lifeboats and they were picked up. They borrowed condoms from the fellows to put their watches in.

We were part of the 5th Canadian Armoured Division. The first equipment we got came from the 5th Regiment Royal Horse Artillery Regiment that had been all across the desert. It was a pile of straight junk. Any good equipment they had, they gave it to their buddies and then dropped off their old crap. Flat tires, no muzzles on the guns, no gun covers. If it

Lt. Sgt. Gordon Bannerman, in dress blues at home on leave from the Royal Canadian Artillery, Christmas 1940.

Bannerman was nineteen when he enlisted, Christmas 1940.

hadn't been for a bunch of prairie farmboys that knew how to get those old Chevs and Fords going, we'd still be there.

We went into the line January 8, 1944, at a place just to the west of Ortona called San Leonardo. That's where we started our war and that's where we had our baptism of fire. It was not too bad at the guns, but our infantry just got absolutely hammered. Our regiment fired eleven thousand rounds that day. The infantry didn't get anywhere. They were up against the German First Paratroops and they just nailed our guys. It was terrible.

We wandered around that area pretty well all winter. We were up in the hills and our infantrymen were very exposed. They supplied the forward line with mules. The Germans could hear them, so they would shell around where the mules were. If our fellows would stop and put a foot in the air, the mules would stop and put a foot in the air too. But when they got where they were going to unload the mules, they had to watch out, because the mules wanted to get the hell out of there right away.

We got through the winter, came down, had a brief rest, and then hit what we called the Hitler Line. That's where I got a bit of shrapnel in my face. It took a little piece out of my cheek. I was sitting under a truck reading a letter from a girl named Audrey from Yellow Grass, Saskatchewan. And, boy, they started the mortars pretty good and I thought, Well, I'd better just roll over on my stomach. So I waited there and the next thing I knew, a shell hit the right front wheel of the truck and blew me up onto my hands and knees. I took off just like a rocket into this stone house, where I was met by the padre. He said, "What's the matter, Gordie?" And I said, "Too damn hot for me." But I didn't lose the letter I was reading. I opened my hand. It was a hot May day and it was just a crumpled ball. I had a pretty good trickle of blood running down my cheek. So the MO put tape on my cheek and that was it. A few days later, I had a scab on my left side, and I picked that off, and there was a shiny bit of steel. Captain Strassen was standing over a little ways, paring his fingernails with his nail file. I asked the MO to take a look. And he took the nail file and flicked it out.

I was a senior sergeant by that time. The Germans had been kicked out of the monastery at Monte Cassino, but they were still in the hills looking right down our backsides. The British Seventy-eighth Division was supposed to clean them out, but they didn't. So we got some terrible shelling in there and my troop just got laced. At Montemaggiore, the amount of shelling we took was unreal. The 48th Highlanders were dug in just ahead of us waiting to make an attack, but they weren't going for two or three days. Tremendous mortaring came down. Hundreds of rounds would come right in on the gun positions and around the 48th. Then a big railway gun started firing at us. It fired a 538-pound shell with a range of thirty-eight miles. It would take a house down pretty good. You'd think it was a freight car going over. They had it on tracks. The Germans would run it out of a tunnel, and fire a round or two, and before your bombers could zero in on it, it would be back in the tunnel. They had a crew of about a hundred. It was some gun.

I saw a lot of deaths, but I remember most this one at Montemaggiore. Young Coyle. The Germans were firing their guns on the town and all of a sudden I saw a stretcher going by and I said, "Who's that?" And they said, "One of yours, Gordie." The big railway gun was firing. Everyone else just sucked in their neck a little bit when one of those shells went over. But the doctor we had was pretty nervous. Coyle went to take his shirt off because it was hot and he was perspiring, and he asked for a shot of morphine. And the doctor said, "If you don't shut up and lie down, you're not going to get anything." So I leaned over Coyle and I said, "Coyle, just lay still a minute." And he said, "I know you, Gordie." And he put his arms up to the back of my neck. And the doctor said, "Leave him. Let him go. Lay him down." And Coyle said, "I'll be quiet." So he gave him a shot. One of the fellows had bandaged Coyle absolutely professionally, but this damned doctor took every one of those bandages off. Then he bandaged him up again and made a hell of a job of it as far as I was concerned. They lowered him into the back of a little truck. And I don't know, we must have all been in a state of shock, because no one went into the back of this little truck with him. I think he was dead by the time he got half a mile down the road. That affected all his really close buddies. They were going to kill that

Bannerman in Riccione, Italy, during the Italian Campaign, October 4, 1944.

doctor. When we got out of the line in November, he was gone the day we came out. So word must have got through to him.

We'd been at Montemaggiore for three or four days before we fired a shot. Then, I think about midnight on August 25, we really let 'er go. You could read a newspaper by the light from the shells going over. The Germans had good intelligence. They knew something was up, so they wanted to get out of there. We caught a whole bunch right out in the open and a lot of them died.

We went into the Gothic Line in August 1944. We were seventy-three days in and we never got out, which is a long time to be within their range. Shellfire is something that you can't get used to. You get frightened. Anyone who says he wasn't frightened was either drunk or wasn't there. It's frightening, because if you let your imagination run, and you hear one of those shells going over, you always visualize that it's got eyes and a nose looking for you. As for the Germans, oh my. When we would let go a barrage of four hundred rounds per gun with about six hundred to seven hundred guns, I used to think about all that coming down on them. One time, we fired about seventy or eighty tons of steel that came down in just a matter of a very few minutes. It was near Monte Cassino. Not too much moved after that.

It took a long, long time for our infantry to realize these beggars were out to kill us. The Germans would make like they were giving themselves up and then they would open fire on the guys coming out to capture them. The Germans had been on the Russian Front, and to shoot somebody didn't mean an awful lot to them. Like shooting a jackrabbit. If you ran into paratroopers or Hitler Youth fellows, that's what they'd learned to do. Kill the enemy. It took a while for us, but we learned too.

In February 1945, we went to Belgium. Once we regrouped and got everyone out of Italy, we were filtered into the line. I was a sergeant major by then. There was this time we came up near a place called Apeldoorn. We were told the Germans were more than thirty miles up the road so we didn't need to dig any gun pits. Then some Dutch people came through and said there were a lot of Germans in the village, just a mile and half away. I rode my motorbike up the road and, God, I had a funny feeling. The hair was riding right up the back of my neck. I felt I was being watched, and I got the hell out of there. When I came back, we dug some trenches all right.

We'd just settled in for the night when the Germans hit us about eleven o'clock. They came down the road right in on top of us. They were everywhere. We couldn't really believe it, that it was happening. One little mortar fluttered in and it hit somebody. Bill Carpenter said, "Who did that hit?" And I said, "Me." I took down my pants and felt around and there was a wee trickle of blood. Just a little pin piece went in, I guess. Freddie Lockhart and I captured one guy. He came around the corner of the house and we both pounced on him. He wasn't armed. His words were, "Nicht shauten, Canadensk. Nicht pistol." ["Don't shoot, Canadian. I don't have a gun."] We got some other prisoners and were looking after them in the house when some Germans ran by and fired. They hit Tom Collin in the hip and shot Ken Nicholson in the stomach. Ken later died.

There were only about forty of us guys. There was another troop behind us, and another across the road. But they were evacuated. We stayed right where we were. I left the command house with another guy to walk toward the guns. And, cripes, we were walking right behind eight or nine Germans pulling a Maxim machine gun on wheels. We grabbed each other. Then he up and ran back to the right, and I veered to the left. The Germans must have heard me or seen me, but they didn't fire. I still don't know why. I ran like a sonofagun to our next gun, and the next gun, and the next gun, to tell them all that the Germans were coming in on them. Even though it was dark, enough buildings were burning that you could see the Germans streaming down the road.

From a distance, at Pop Barkwell's gun, I heard them give the challenge. Then there were a few machine-gun shots and screams, which kept on pretty good for a while and then there was quiet. I found out later that old Pop Barkwell was knocking them down with his bare fists. I guess he just got so damn upset that they had nerve enough to come that close. Those he didn't punch out, the guys shot. Two of the crew shot two Germans that were within a foot of their rifles. The Germans crawled up to get a shot at them, I guess, as they were lying on their backs in their slit trenches. The guys just poked the rifles out and nailed them. In the morning, there were dead and dying Germans all around them.

The Germans captured one of our fellows, a guy named Iverson. They held him all night. They took his boots and socks off, and they said, "If we get chased out of here, we're not going to take you with us. We're going to

Troop Sgt. Maj. Gordon Bannerman (left) and Sgt. Orme Payne, shortly after seventy-three days in action without being relieved by another unit.

Bannerman (right) and Payne in 2002, sixty years after they enlisted in the Canadian Armed Forces together.

shoot you." So when a flame thrower came through and the flames hit, Iverson grabbed one of their revolvers and captured a few of them. Daylight finally came, of course, and the fighting ended. But it had been a bad night. They were right in on top of us. They were everywhere.

All night I had wondered what had happened to my friend Orme Payne. We joined up together and we'd been right through the war together. I saw the house at battery headquarters where he would have been go up in fire during the night. And I thought, Well . . . Later, I was walking across a field and saw someone coming toward me. It was Orme. He said, "God, I'm glad to see you, Gordie. I had heard that you'd been killed." And I said, "Yeah, I'm sure glad to see you too."

"After we passed Aix-la-Chapelle,
we lost about twenty-two aircraft
in twenty minutes, all going down
in flames. It was scary. We never
thought we'd reach our target."

JIM MOFFAT

JIM MOFFAT

I was twenty when I joined the air force. I never went to high school, so I didn't have enough education to be a pilot. But they said I could be an air gunner. I thought, That's aircrew. I'll take it. I graduated second in our course. You have to be able to recognize aircraft and you have to be able to shoot fairly accurately and you have to be stupid. The death rate among gunners was about twice that of the rest of the crew. On the third or fourth day I was in England, they asked for volunteers to go straight to the squadron rather than extra training. Four of us volunteered. I went to 427 Squadron. In a week or two, we made our first op.

It was September 5, 1943. We were flying a Halifax bomber to Mannheim. [Moffat was the mid-upper gunner.] About fifty miles from the target, we lost a motor. The wing was flapping, and the pilot was panicking. "Where the hell is the engineer?" The engineer was very cool and calm. He said, "I'm right here and we're taking care of it." He eventually got the motor feathered, and we were able to go across the target. It was thrilling. The second night was uneventful, and the third night we got shot up. We were just crossing the coast. We knew the fighter was there.

Moffat's crew at a debriefing. Moffat is at the back, far right, facing the camera.

We were weaving and trying to get off his track, but he gave it the whole shot and set the bomb load on fire. He killed the rear gunner and the wireless op, and badly wounded the engineer. The pilot put it into a dive. The fire went out and we flew back home. Cardy, the engineer, had been hit in the eye and the arm by a 29 mm shell. He was lying on the floor. They bandaged him up and gave him some morphine.

When we got back to base, we couldn't get the wheels down. The ground crew said, "Aim it out to sea and everybody jump out by parachute." And the pilot said, "I can't do that because I have a wounded man on board. I'm going to land." Cardy came to and we told him we couldn't get the wheels down. He told us to take him to the middle of the aircraft, and he'd show us what wires to cut. We cut them, and the wheels came down. When we landed, the plane burst into flames, but the fire trucks were there. Cardy got the conspicuous gallantry medal. The pilot, George Laird, got the DFC. It was the only DFC on our squadron that went to a Canadian in the war. We were about one-third British. The tail gunner that died had been my roommate. I didn't really react until the next day. I went to talk to a couple of my buddies about it. Two days later, I heard that they crashed while coming in off a training trip and both of them were killed.

On March 30–31, 1944, we got the op on Nuremburg. [Moffat was a tail gunner then.] It was in moonlight and everyone thought, Holy hell, we're all for the chop. You never operated in Germany in moonlight because it was too dangerous. But Harris [head of Bomber Command] wanted one more raid before he turned things over to Eisenhower to concentrate on railway yards. After we passed Aix-la-Chapelle, we lost about twenty-two aircraft in twenty minutes, all going down in flames. It was scary. We never thought we'd reach our target. But no planes were going down near us. We were glad the moon had gone by the time we got there. We were right over the target when we let the bombs go.

We thought we were home safe. But the navigator forgot to correct the course because of the winds and after about an hour, he said, "Sorry, skipper. I've made an error. I'll give you a corrected course shortly." After another hour, I heard the pilot say, "What the hell?" and there was a loud crash. I knew what had happened. We had hit another aircraft. I looked to my right and everything was okay. I looked to my left and there was no tail section! It had broken off. So I thought, I'm getting out. I was able to stand halfway out of the aircraft because most of the roof had been torn away. I got up on the side of the turret and jumped out into the darkness. I pulled my hand away from the parachute and it opened. After swinging three or four times, I hit the ground. I learned later that I was the only survivor of the two planes. I don't know why the navigator, the wireless op, and the bomb aimer didn't get out. They're down below the pilot and the bottom of our aircraft had been okay. Four got out from the other plane. One landed in a tree and he was speared to death by the branches. The chutes of the other three didn't open. I guess they didn't get out early enough.

I landed about 3:30 in the morning. I was tired. I picked up my chute, walked into a forest, rolled up, and went to sleep. In the morning, I got to a village and at the end of it, there were four guys with bicycles and they said, "Prisoneer! Prisoneer!" And I thought, Oh hell, they're going to turn me over to the Germans. But then a fellow ran up behind them and said, "I'm from Birmingham and I'm here to get you back into England. Get behind the bloody hedge. The Germans are right behind you." So I got behind the hedge. It started snowing. It was all so unreal. I think I must have been in a state of shock. I did everything automatically. That was about 10 a.m. and no one came for me until just before dark. Then, one of the men pointed me to this forest where two gendarmes were waiting. I thought they were going to arrest me, but they were in the Belgian Resistance. The next day, we drove forty miles north to a place called Attal. Jones, an English airman, was also with us. We stayed in the gendarme's home for six weeks, learning French. His name was Albert Paul. We slept upstairs. They had a blanket separating us from where they were sleeping. We were not allowed out. We had a Sten gun they'd given us. Albert said, "If there are two or three Germans, you shoot them and you run. If there are more than that, forget the gun. Just run."

It didn't happen that way. The Germans came about six in the morning when we were still sleeping. I woke up to see Jones jumping out the window, and I heard someone screaming, "Les Boches! Les Boches!" I could hear them breaking the door down. I didn't know that Albert had already been captured by the Gestapo. I pulled my pants on and jumped out the window. Jones was about a hundred feet ahead of me. As we were getting out into the field, the Germans were up in the window shooting. I found out that rifle bullets make a humming noise like a bee as they go by. And others don't make any noise until they hit the ground. The bullets went right into the ground in front of me. I thought, "How the hell did they miss my legs?" I yelled to Jones, "Let's go down to the hedge." Either he didn't hear me or he panicked. He was shot in the leg and captured. By this time, the Germans had gone out the back door and were shooting at

Moffat (right) and Fl./Lt. Neville Murray.

Murray took over when Moffat's crew went missing.

*Sous notre drapeau surmonté de la Croix,
on peut mourir, on n'est pas vaincu.* (L. Veuillot)

Albert PAUL
né à Torgny le 7 Juin 1915
Maréchal des logis de Gendarmerie à Étalle
Invalide de guerre 1940
Chef de Bataillon des Partisans du F. I.
tombé à Liége sous les balles du peloton d'exécution
le 14 Août 1944.

Papeterie J. Diderich-Scharff, Messancy

Courtesy Jim Moffat

Albert Paul's 1944 funeral program. Paul was held in a Gestapo prison in Liege on charges of aiding downed Allied airmen, and was shot on August 14.

me with one of the Sten guns. The bullets were hitting the barbed wire along the hedge. I dove under the barbed wire and my pants got caught. I just left them there and ran. I thought I would be okay as soon as I got to the forest. But there was no undergrowth. I thought I was finished. I was breathing like a steam engine. I jumped into a bush. Of course it was a thorn bush, so I scratched myself a bit. But my adrenalin was running so high, I didn't feel any pain. They scoured the forest looking for me. I could see one German's legs go by, but he couldn't find me. I slept there that night.

After the war, Jones wrote a letter to Albert Paul's brother Vital and told him what happened. Jones said the Germans thought he was a spy and was going to shoot him, but Albert said, "He's an airman." That saved his life. But they beat the hell out of them for two or three weeks. Then they shipped them to the citadel at Liege, and gave them another treatment. Vital was allowed to see his brother a month after he was taken prisoner. He told his wife, "He's in such bad shape. I can't go back. I'll never go back." They shipped Jones to a POW camp. Albert stayed at Liege until three days before the Americans liberated it. Then the Germans took all the prisoners out, a hundred and some, and shot them. It was terrible. Unbelievable. Albert was the guy who saved me.

I was on the loose and I was lost. A fellow in a field with some sheep gave me a pail of water and pointed to a haystack. "You can sleep here." I could tell he was scared stiff. I woke up next morning and he was yelling, "You have a friend." I looked up and saw a little man walking along, head hunched over to one side, wearing the usual big Belgian beret and a green uniform. He was a forester. And he said, "I am Desiré Paul, cousin of Albert and Vital Paul. I'm here to take you back into Belgium." Apparently I'd walked into France. So he took me back to the Pauls' family home. It was unbelievable they were still helping people.

I stayed there for a while in a tiny room under the steeple in a little church that was used as a museum. I slept on a pallet of straw. On weekends, we'd go out into the forest and look for beetles because Desiré collected them for the museum. Then I became very ill because my scratches had become infected and I was malnourished. I was only eating one meal a day and not drinking much water. I couldn't sleep. I asked for a doctor. So they took me away to this Resistance camp and a doctor there gave me a shot of something. I passed out for a while, and that gave everyone a scare.

A few weeks after that, I decided to head for Switzerland. In France, I ran into a Resistance guy who said he would take me to his home and within a short time they would fly me to England. Great, I thought. On the way, he took me into a forest and introduced me to twenty young men, not very well armed. They were his Resistance group.

Later that day, we were in his home and his wife started screaming, "Les Boches!" And he said, "There's the window. You don't know me. Get out now! Don't come back." I ran out the back and there was a big hedge. I was getting down to crawl under it and I saw a pair of boots and a rifle butt on the other side. So I froze. I didn't move for at least an hour. Eventually a truck picked them up and the Germans disappeared. I waited until midnight. It was a bright moonlit night. I thought I could find my way back to the Resistance camp. Sure enough, I found the trail. I walked in and everyone was lying down, sleeping. I called out, "Hello. Hello." No one answered. I went over, touched them. Cold as ice. The Germans had been following us and shot them all. They didn't have a chance to run or anything. That's the one time I lost my cool. I just turned around and ran.

The next day I was walking along and I heard voices. "Bonjour," I said. And they stuck rifles in my nose. It was the Resistance. The Germans liked to use plants posing as airmen and I had no identification. They said, "If you are not who you say you are, we won't waste a bullet. We'll just string you up." One of the guys played a mouth organ. I asked to borrow it and tried to play "Irish Washerwoman" or something like that. I heard them say, "I think he may be a Canadian. A German wouldn't play until he could do it properly." A few days later, three people came in, questioned me for an hour, and they said I was okay. Everyone shook my hand. Hugs and kisses.

Three days later, we heard there were either Americans or Germans in the village. Four of us went to check. I looked into the square and here's a sergeant with his feet over the windshield, and I thought, Well, that's an American. The Germans would never do that. It was a reconnaissance group. They gave me a spare uniform and an automatic pistol and we all took off looking for bridges to see if they were mined. Eventually we saw one in the distance and there was an inn nearby. The sergeant said, "You speak French. Go ask if there are any Germans around." And the people said, "Oh yes. Be careful. The Germans are on the other side of the river." The lieutenant said, "Oh, they're full of it." So here we were charging fifty miles an hour toward this bridge. I know it's full of Germans and I know they're going to start shooting. About halfway to the bridge, they open up. I don't know to this day how they missed us. I think the shells were about four feet to our left. You could hear them tearing through the air. Just like someone ripping tar paper. They fired six shots by the time we turned around and called in air support.

A few days later, a small Auster plane landed and they flew me back to England. I was in such bad shape they put me in hospital for a couple of weeks. I'd been on the loose for five and a half months. Any day could have been my last. I was 160 pounds when I was shot down and 125 when I got back to England. The thing I think about most is what happened to those twenty people in the Resistance camp. If we had not stopped to say hello, maybe they'd still be alive. But you have to put it aside, or you go crazy.

"There's no place
in the world that
gets as dark as
it gets at sea."

JOHN DOYLE

JOHN DOYLE

I served in the Royal Canadian Naval Voluntary Reserve on a minesweeper in the North Atlantic. There were no heroics. I made many trips to the rail to throw up, seasick. Sometimes I still had my pencil in my hand when I was interrupted from my deciphering, while fighting the fearsome elements of the North Atlantic winter gales. For young Canadian sailors, it was an endurance test of a lifetime.

I joined the Royal Canadian Navy at their recruiting station in Ottawa on July 23, 1942. The air force wouldn't accept me for poor vision or something. At the time, I had never seen anything bigger than a little tug on the Rideau River. The war was getting very serious by then. We were drafted to HM Signal School at Saint-Hyacinthe, Quebec, for rigorous training in communications. Since the war was going badly for us, it was necessary to have us trained and available at Halifax for assignment to our ships as soon as possible.

I was deciphering and coding. I worked with a machine, a modified Enigma version that the British got from the Germans. It's okay to talk

John Doyle, Acting Leading Coder for the Royal Canadian Navy, in Nova Scotia, 1943, at twenty years of age.

Courtesy John Doyle

The HMCS *Digby*, pendant number J267, Bangor Class Minesweeper, 1942.

about it after all these years, but it was highly secure then. It was like a big typing machine. You typed in, I think there were five-figure groups, and they came out in plain English. As soon as I got the message decoded, I'd take the signal to the bridge, to the officer of the day, and he would decide whether we should wake the captain, if it was at night, and let him see the signal, and I'd go back to my work. Maybe I'd stop at the rail on the way. Anyway, that was communications.

I was at Stadacona Barracks in Halifax trying to find my way around the base when a runner came to me with a draft notice instructing me to join the HMCS *Digby*, a minesweeper, at 2300 hours. I was told we would take seven other naval escort vessels with us to New York without a convoy and likely pick up a convoy there. (We were part of Halifax Escort Group Five.) We passed through the open gates of Halifax Harbour. The gates consisted of cable nets supported by floats. The nets went to the bottom

Doyle took this photo shipside during a torpedo operation off the HMCS *Digby*, 1942.

of the harbour and had explosives connected to them. They crossed the mouth of the harbour and were pulled open and closed by tugs. I went up on deck to see what I could see. The city lights were low and quickly faded as we increased speed to fourteen knots. I began to feel queasy with the groundswell, as well as the stiff southwest wind that we were heading into. Our bow was going up, up, up and then down, down, down. Water was flying everywhere over the ship. The first lieutenant informed me that we were now at the front and could see action any minute.

The ship was not equipped with minesweeping gear. It had been changed to do corvette work, convoy escort work, because it became clear the Atlantic seaboard was not going to be covered with mines. A corvette was like a trawler or a fishing boat. It was a great ship for the rough seas. It was a fair size, about three hundred feet long. We had a four-inch gun on the bow and twin machine guns on both wings of the bridge. We had a pom-pom aircraft gun on the stern on the rear gun mount. But we only used our guns for target practice. Our main weapon was the depth charge. They were three-hundred-pound canisters. We'd set them to roll off from the rails at the stern. We'd pre-set them to explode at a certain depth where you thought the U-boat would be. The intense concussion from exploding depth charges would blow my flimsy earphones right off my head and lift the stern of the ship out of the water.

It was a difficult trip to New York against a brisk wind, but we finally tied up at Staten Island Pier Number 9 alongside several Canadian warships. On shore leave, we made our way to Broadway and shows put on by the USO. We even met a few movie stars. As we departed the huge harbour at night into open water, there were high winds and it was very, very rough. A big battleship cut across our bow and just missed us. I don't know how it happened. If we had been struck, that thing would have cut us right in two. We think it was the USS *Texas*. It just emerged right in front of us. The crew on the bridge were terrified. For some reason, they didn't see us. Their radar didn't pick us up and our radar failed in that wind. There's no place in the world that gets as dark as it gets at sea. We were lucky.

It was our job to take a position around the large convoys of merchant ships. There might be twenty rows of them, maybe more, and we would be three thousand yards away on either the port or starboard side. The merchant ships would be six hundred yards ahead of each other, with a destroyer four thousand yards ahead of the nearest freighter. We would zigzag to and from the convoy. We would go way, way out, maybe twenty miles from the convoy, and hustle right back. We wanted to cover as much area as possible to make sure there were no U-boats lurking near the convoy. We had to move very fast and in rough water. That's what made it so bad, when you have to open up high speed and plough through those waves. I don't know how we survived those ferocious storms and the icy spray from sixty-foot waves. Sometimes, when there was a change of course, the vessel would fall into a trough. We would momentarily lie on our side. This caused great suspense, especially for those who would have been sleeping and not warned.

We spent long days and nights on the constant lookout for U-boats. The German submariner fought with awesome tenacity. Unknown to us at the time, there were seventy-five to one hundred U-boats operating in the western Atlantic. The Black Pit was the graveyard for many sinkings. It started about five hundred miles east of Newfoundland. The Germans had a heyday there, because they knew covering aircraft could not go that far. They would line across and go hunting without much effort. Merchant ships took a terrible beating. The U-boat could do forty knots and fire a torpedo from two hundred feet below the surface at a seven-mile range. They could be twenty feet below in thirty seconds and seven hundred feet below in one minute. The German U-boat commander could see the silhouettes of the ships for miles by looking down moon. But looking into the dark, we had to spot a tiny periscope. It was impossible. There were 1,450 Canadian merchant seamen killed and 750 merchant ships sunk in the first year and a half.

They were all difficult trips with many action station calls, but we never saw any U-boats. They always kept out of sight. But there would be frequent pings from our asdic detection gear, and that required depth charges. We were junior officers on the escort, so we got the less attractive job of breaking off from our convoy and proceeding to the last known location of a U-boat. We would be sitting ducks, but the submarine would always have dived and be long gone when we got there. Then, we had to race back to rejoin the convoy.

The U-boats didn't scare us too much. It was the storms that really scared us. Don't forget we were all twenty years old. Sometimes you'd get in your hammock and you'd wonder, Is there anything heading for us?

Our communications
staff on board HMCS
Digby at sea

Crew photo of the HMCS *Digby* communications staff, 1942.
Doyle is in the top row, second from the left.

What am I going to do if we get hit? The first thing you'd do is leap from
the hammock and try to grab a life jacket and head to the upper deck, and
jump if need be. It would always come to your mind in those freezing
waters that you're going to have to take a jump to survive.

Many of us got seasick. We had ninety men on board and I think the
captain was the only one who didn't get sick. It's the pitch that really gets
to you. A stern sea is no problem and the roll is no problem. It was heading into that almighty wind that was the problem. I would be in the wireless cabin and have to drop everything and run. I was seasick many, many
times. It was embarrassing.

Late in 1944, we were pulled off the Halifax Force because of new losses in the Gulf of St. Lawrence. The German U-boat was in the Gulf and it was a constant threat to shipping. The Battle of the Gulf of St. Lawrence is a little-known phase of the Second World War. Yet it took place right within Canada. There were quite a few merchant ships sunk on the way down from Montreal. And a few warships too. Many men were lost. The U-boats claim they went within a hundred miles of Quebec City. They'd lie in wait, right off the Canadian shores, for those convoys to come down. They had some pretty smart submariners. They'd get in at the Strait of Belle Isle and they might get out at the Cabot Straits. Defending the convoys and shores of the Gulf of St. Lawrence was exhausting work. We made several trips from Sydney to the Gaspé and into the St. Lawrence River to escort merchant ships up and down. It was winter and it could get really rough. The weather was usually terrible. Snowstorms and everything else.

One night in November, on a cold, stormy approach to the mouth of the St. Lawrence, we received pings on our asdic monitor. It was a U-boat. Action stations were called at 9:30 in the evening. We were now in close contact with the submarine. We went into a severe manoeuvre to avoid being torpedoed and we started dropping depth charges at predetermined settings for explosions. In order to be lethal, the depth charge must explode within twenty feet of the hardened-steel inner hull of the U-boat. The U-boat would dive to avoid our depth-charge patterns and frequently discharge oil smudges to the surface to try to deceive us. He would keep diving and then he'd try to surface again. But we could pick him up as soon as he came within a certain range and we'd start depth charging and send him back down again. It was cat and mouse. We were at action stations all night long, every time the submarine would try to get into firing position. The attacks went on until 6:30 in the morning. It was the longest attack we faced. Usually, attacks in the open Atlantic lasted about twenty minutes before we'd lose contact. We finally exhausted our supply of depth charges and had to go to Rimouski in a howling snowstorm to replenish. When we got back to where we had been, there was no more contact. He had dived to deeper depths. The U-boat

Winter patrols on the HMCS *Digby*, northwest Atlantic, 1943.

was gone. We did not think we made the kill. This was later substantiated by naval intelligence.

After we had been back in Sydney for a few days, we were called out at night. The HMCS *Shawinigan*, a corvette, was missing in heavy seas in the Cabot Straits. We went out and started calling for many hours. No answer. We later learned the sad truth. It was torpedoed by a U-boat. Ninety-some men lost. They eventually found seven bodies floating on the surface. Some were personal friends. Before that, I always felt safe from torpedoing in heavy seas. But that got rid of any such comfort I might have felt.

The crest for the Royal Canadian
Navy personnel who served
on board the HMCS *Digby*
in the northwest Atlantic.

I was two years at sea. We never got hit. The *Esquimalt* was close to us when it was torpedoed and sunk. The *Clayoquot* was sunk too, and, of course, the *Shawinigan*. One of my friends was being transferred when his boat got cut in two in the St. Lawrence River. He survived.

Some day, when you're flying over the north Atlantic, look down through the gaps in the clouds and see an enormous battlefield where the longest, bloodiest, decisive battle in all history took place. It was the Battle of the Atlantic, 1939–45.

"All of a sudden, every battleship,
destroyer, every ship that had a gun
started to bombard the beaches.
The smoke and the flames and the
roar were overwhelming."

GORDON HENDERY

GORDON HENDERY

I joined the navy as an ordinary seaman in 1941. After three months, I was sent out to naval college in Esquimalt on Vancouver Island. Ten of us lads that graduated volunteered for Royal Naval Commandos because we were told we could go overseas immediately. We wanted to be in the thick of things. Don't forget we were kids, eighteen and nineteen. So we came home, had ten days' leave in Montreal, and I got engaged to a lovely girl there. We're still married. When we got to Glasgow, we were told we weren't going to be commandos. We were going to be combined operations. We would be operating the landing craft that would take boys onto the beaches. It sounded exciting, and it proved to be far more exciting than we ever dreamed.

We finally joined a convoy out of Liverpool in March 1943. We didn't know where we were going, but they lashed our twelve landing craft on top of three merchant ships and headed to sea. Off the coast of Portugal, we ran into submarines. The wolf pack was in the middle of the convoy and they couldn't miss. We lost four ships all around us. Ahead of us, to

Lt. Comdr. Gordon Hendery of the Royal Canadian Navy in Corfu, Greece, Christmas 1944.

the stern of us. We were just waiting for it. But it didn't happen. I was up top during it all and there was a funny noise on the bridge. I said to Johnny Walker, my warrant officer, "Johnny, what's that?" And he said, "I'm sorry, sir. It's my knees knocking." You had to laugh sometimes.

We couldn't go past Gibraltar into the Mediterranean because it wasn't safe. So we went right down to Cape Town, South Africa, a beautiful city. Then we headed to Aden and then to the Red Sea. That was marvellous. No submarines. No planes. You could smoke on deck. But, my gosh, it was hot. We were sitting out one day, and I said, "Bring an egg over here." I scraped the paint off the deck, put the egg down, and it fried up perfectly. We got to Port Tufik, a little city at the bottom of the Suez Canal, and they ordered us to launch all our landing craft in the water. We were going up to Alexandria, through the Suez Canal. I said, "You've got to be kidding." It took us four or five days. Once, in the middle of the night, we heard whoop, whoop, whoop. We turned around and there's a bloody great battleship, the [Royal Navy's] *Warspite*. So we pulled over as close to the bank as we could, because we thought she would swamp us. As it went by, all their guys lined the railing and threw us cigarettes, chocolate bars, and oranges. It was wonderful. When we got to Port Said, we went to the bar, and I don't think any of us have ever had a cold beer we enjoyed more in our life.

We finished up in Alexandria and set sail again. The captain called me to his cabin. "Lieutenant Hendery. You'd like to know. You're going to the landing in Sicily." That was the first I knew of it. There was another big convoy and we had our landing craft lashed up again on merchant ships. On July 9, a big transport plane flew over, towing gliders filled with British paratroopers. We knew they had a job to do before us. The next morning, it was a horrible sight. A lot of the parachutes were in the water with boys drowned on the end of them. We even had to slow the ship so we wouldn't bump into them. It was terrible.

The boys landed in a little town called Avola. There were casualties, but nothing like D-Day. There were more Italians there than Germans, and the Italians didn't have the heart for the war. We took our landing craft up to the city of Syracusa. We went back and forth from the cargo

Courtesy Gordon Hendery

A photo taken by Hendery of the preparation for the landing on D-Day, June 6, 1944.

ships with all the ammunition and food supplies and everything the army needed. This was the first time the landing craft had really been used. They worked extremely well. Once, we were unloading ammunition, and the captain and I were up on board having a chat. All of a sudden a German plane flew over and we saw a bomb coming down. We went flat on our bellies and the bomb landed in the water and sprayed shrapnel all over our ship and some other ships. One ship was on fire and I could see a lot of boys leaping into the water. I jumped into my craft and we dashed over. By that time, the water was on fire with gasoline. We went right through a wall of flames and picked up all the boys in the water. Then we turned around and went through the flames again.

It took thirty-eight days to capture Sicily. There was some very heavy fighting. The Germans just didn't want to give up. We lost quite a few boys. Then we had to meet up with our Canadians, take them across the Strait of Messina to Italy. But along the way, I had an attack of malaria and dysentery. I was sick as a poisoned pup. I spent a couple of weeks in a hospital in Tunisia. When I was released, I had nothing on but my battledress. No flotilla. No nothing. But what the hell, I was young and I recuperated quickly. I went to the colonel, and he said, "I've got something for you, young man. Here's a jeep. It's only got two cylinders, but it's working." So I took the jeep, drove to Algiers, and I was able to hitchhike on a ship back to England. I was told to join HMCS *Prince Henry* in Glasgow. She was an LSI troop ship, Landing Ship Infantry.

The Canadian Scottish Regiment from Vancouver joined us and a few days later came a New Brunswick regiment. We knew we were going to land somewhere soon, but we didn't know where. Finally we were told the landing was going to be Normandy. On the night of June 5, we gave all the boys a hot dinner. I didn't get any sleep that night. I was excited. As I walked up and down, officers were in our cabins, writing letters to their loved ones. In the morning, we had breakfast at four o'clock.

Finally, the boys were up on deck, opposite their landing craft. We issued them all vomit bags, because we knew some of them would be seasick. We boarded the craft, loaded them in the water, and, was it ever rough. It was awful. We were about four miles from the beach. All of a sudden, every battleship, destroyer, every ship that had a gun started to bombard the beaches. The smoke and the flames and the roar were overwhelming. And the boys on the craft said this was going to be a picnic if they were going to bombard the beach like that. But we knew damn well from experience that whenever we got to a beach, there was enemy fire to greet us.

The landing craft were only about three feet above the water. They could toss about a lot. They had a half-inch steel plate around them. The boys were loaded on the deep side of the landing craft under the deck, so they wouldn't get wet. But it was very, very choppy. Fear and seasickness from the rich dinner the night before and everything else all accumulated

Courtesy Gordon Hendery

Troops make practice runs as part of their training for D-Day.

to make them sick as could be. They were so happy to have the vomit bags. There were thirty soldiers to a craft. Some had machine guns. They all had rifles and sixty-pound packs. They must have been terrified, but you know, they were trained for this. They were soldiers.

On the way in, a wonderful thing happened. A young sergeant got up on the deck beside me and started to sing a song, "Roll out the Barrel." Everyone joined in. It was one of the most moving experiences I had during my almost five years in the service. There was fear on everyone's faces, and he tried to brighten up their spirits. I was in the same fix. I was human too. And it worked. The fear left our faces.

Then we saw these nasty spikes that came up out of the water. They had mines on the ends of them. We knew if we touched one we'd be blown

Courtesy Gordon Hendery

The Canadian Scottish Regiment's landing on D-Day, June 6, 1944.

to smithereens. We wanted to get the boys landed on dry sod, but the craft got stuck on an obstacle under the water. Just think how the boys felt: seasick, packs on their backs, being splashed from machine-gun bullets beside the craft. I hesitated to order "down doors," but it had to be done. They jumped into the water. Some were up to the waist. Two of the shorter lads jumped in and didn't come up. Terrible. They only had twenty feet of water to go through, but it was deep. And there was not a damn thing we could do, because our orders were to get out of the way and back on the ship as quickly as possible. Those thirty guys got out in one heck of a hurry. They dashed across the beach. Some fell from machine-gun fire. Some were hit before they even made the beach. We could see all this. Imagine training in England for three years and not even being able to get to the beach before being killed. I don't think people realize what our boys did.

When we got back to the ship, Scott Young was on board. He was a reporter, I think, from the *Globe and Mail*. He asked me what happened. I told him everything and he passed this on to Matthew Halton, who was a Canadian radio reporter [CBC]. And when they announced the Normandy landing, they referred to our ship and my name was mentioned. So my family knew I was safe.

After that, we were ordered to southern France for a landing that was completely American. Special Service boys. We towed them in on rubber rafts to Port Cros Island, which had to be captured before we could do anything to the beaches. I could see the machine-gun bullets going over our heads as we landed them. But they did their job beautifully. On the way back to the ship, we saw a young guy on the beach waving his arms, so we went back. It was an American sergeant and he had ten German prisoners with him. He said, "Sir, could you take these prisoners off my hands? I don't know what to do with them." I said okay and I handed him a receipt that said, Received ten prisoners on board, with the date on it and his name. Kernaghan or something. The prisoners were terrified. They thought we were going to shoot them. They showed us pictures of their families. We were on our way to Corsica to pick up ammunition, guns, bombs, and shells, and we dumped those prisoners there.

We took this ammunition to the partisans fighting against the Germans in Greece. We had to land it at three o'clock in the morning. As my craft was loaded in the water, I saw a light shining from the beach. And I said, "I bet that's for us." We followed it, and it was one of the partisans waiting for our ammunition. We shook hands and got back to the ship. Well, thirty-odd years later, my wife and I were at a hotel restaurant in Dubrovnik, Yugoslavia. The waiter's name was Joseph, a nice white-haired chap. He and I started to talk about the war. I told him about being in Greece, and he said, "Sir, when you landed the craft, did you see a light? Well, I was holding the light." I damn near choked and he almost dropped the plate. It was the most amazing coincidence. The people in the dining room heard the chat and they all started to applaud.

German soldiers captured by the Allies on Juno Beach, June 7, 1944.

We also went to Piraeus, the port for Athens. The British officers there asked us to take in a group of Ghurkas from Nepal. They were short guys and absolutely fearless. Each one carried a knife about two feet long and it was sharp. If they took it out of their scabbard, they had to draw blood, even if they just cut their own finger. We came back to pick them up. When they got on board, they opened their hands and they had ears as souvenirs.

The second day we had to round the harbour again and I came to a little town where fishermen were mending their nets. They all crowded around and the villagers also came down. I took a picture of us, with me in the middle of it. There was a donkey in there too. Eventually, I received orders to report back to London, and I joined another convoy going to Canada.

Many years later, my wife and I were on a visit to Greece and we found out we were just four kilometres from that same little town. So we drove there, and as I got out of the car, an old man with a black beret and a black coat, pushing a bicycle with a box full of grapes on the back, was passing by. A lot of Greeks speak French, so I said to him, "Excusez moi, monsieur . . ." And I had in my hand the picture of the group from 1945. He looked and said, "C'est moi." The hair started to stand up on the back of my neck. He ran into the little taverna there, and a lot of those guys came out. They looked at the picture and they said, "We're all here, but the donkey's dead." They all laughed. I looked at my wife and I said, "There's the circle and the knot has been tied."

"We left from Halifax sometime in March 1944. We were told it was the largest armada to ever cross the ocean. On a clear day, I could see ships almost horizon to horizon."

HUGH NEILY

HUGH NEILY

When the war started, I was on a farm just outside Middleton, Nova Scotia, in the Annapolis Valley. I enlisted in March 1941. I wasn't quite old enough, but a lot us were underage. I spent two years in the Medical Corps. I quickly moved up from corporal to sergeant and was running the main office of a 125-bed hospital. But it wasn't my idea of what the army was. I took a combination of IQ and aptitude tests called the M Test. If you got a certain score, you just might become an officer. That's what happened in my case. They put me in infantry and I enjoyed it. In December 1943, the call came from Britain. They were short of infantry officers, and they needed volunteers. That's how I got overseas quickly and into the British Army.

We left from Halifax sometime in March 1944. We were told it was the largest armada to ever cross the ocean. On a clear day, I could see ships almost horizon to horizon. We ran into terrible storms. Several of those liberty boats just disappeared overnight, the seas were so rough. We

Infantry Officer Hugh Neily of the 2nd Battalion East Yorkshire Regiment and the 3rd British Infantry Division in summer uniform at the Canadian Basic Training Centre in Yarmouth, Nova Scotia, 1943.

were at sea for sixteen days, zigzagging back and forth. I ended up with the East Yorkshire Regiment. They were a pretty likeable bunch, and I determined that I would be close with them. I would sit and talk with them and find out where they came from. In fact, I still have a list of all my men.

We weren't told where D-Day was going to happen, or when. But we were advised to be ready for early summer. They had low-flying planes going in at wavetop, taking pictures of the landing area. They did that at about a dozen different places, so the Germans would never catch on. The photos showed the buildings, machine-gun pits, sandbag strong points, slit trenches, wire entanglements, minefield outlines, telegraph poles, and so on. I was given the task of building a huge model of our company's landing site from the photos. It took us three days. We built it on a slope so we could lie down and see the landmarks we should be able to see from the water when we came in to land. As it turned out, on the actual approach, we were able to see from several hundred feet out, so the model was a tremendous asset.

Our ship was the *Glenearn*, a troop ship. We stayed there overnight before the landing, and someone came round and said, "Winnie's here! Winnie's here!" I went up on deck and sure enough, there was Churchill standing in a launch, with cigar and bowler hat. Standing right beside him was a skinny little guy, Jan Christian Smuts [prime minister of South Africa]. Churchill waved his cigar at us, and that was the biggest excitement of that day.

Leaving the harbour that night is the one thing in my life that I will never forget. As far as you could see in every direction, nothing but boats. Nobody went to sleep. We were all leaning on the rail, watching. But we couldn't even see lights over there. Just a dark, low coastline. We had a huge breakfast at three o'clock in the morning. Bacon and eggs, which was a real rarity. We had to put blacking on our faces. We had a different helmet than regular infantry. It was very large, so we heard kind of an echo when we walked. It was covered in netting that we called scrim. We put pieces of burlap in the scrim to take away the roundness so there was no silhouette to give us away. We were ready.

When the ship stopped, we knew we were off the coast of France. Watches were synchronized, checked and rechecked, along with the rifles, the Bren guns, the Sten guns, the ammunition pouches. Off in the distance we could hear very heavy firing and bombardment where the planes were going over. Day was breaking fast and the waves were very high. We were the first ones to go down. Colonel Hutchinson came on the loud hailer and wished us all luck. He said, "I want you to repeat after me: 'It all depends on me.'" So we all repeated that. It was very tricky getting in the LCA because the waves were high. But we made it all right and we pulled away. We lined up four abreast, and on the far side, there was B Company, also four. So we went in eight ahead. We were followed in three minutes by C and D Companies. And behind them other companies were coming in. Christ, you gotta get in there, get landed, and get through those defences in three minutes so the next wave can come in after you. That's how tight it was.

There was a terrible noise all the way in. Navy boats were firing shell after shell. They would fire a broadside from one side, turn, then fire from the other side. The noise was tremendous. And planes were going over. If there was a sky, we couldn't see it. The German shells started coming too. When we landed, there were these beach defences. [Timber posts were cocked at a seaward angle with twenty-pound Teller mines attached to their tops.] If you hit one, it would blow the front of the ship off. But we made it okay. I got my men out, and I dashed forward. Then flat on the sand. There were no other footprints. We were first. My men followed me off and immediately spread to the right. Within thirty seconds of landing, one of my men went down. I heard someone say, "Oh God. Billy's been shot." He was dead before he hit the ground. A bullet right in his head.

I looked to the left. Nothing moving there. I looked to the right, and I went over to my sergeant and said, "I'm going to go in. Follow my tracks." So I ran straight forward to where this machine-gun post was. My runner was right behind me, carrying the wire cutters. We cut the wire in just seconds, a section about eight feet wide. We'd practised this. And I crawled up the dunes. I can still feel those little reedy grasses on my face. Because of the model, I knew exactly where the machine gun was. The post was circular, about eight feet in diameter. And right in the centre, there was a spike on which they had mounted a machine gun. I could see the damn thing, but it wasn't moving. I crawled up on my belly as close as I could, reached back and got a grenade. I tossed it and it hit the concrete parapet and rolled. My first reaction was, For God's sake, don't go down there and kill them. My next reaction was, You damn fool. That's why you're here. It exploded right on the parapet, and immediately a white flag came up. But nothing happened. So I fired one round and four fellows came out. They were the sorriest excuse for soldiers I'd ever seen. I thought, My God, is this what we're fighting? They stood there with their hands behind the back of their heads. Then they sat down and we left them behind.

I got to the road, signalling to all my fellows to hurry up and get through. We got to a ditch on the other side and the major gave the order to proceed. We hadn't gone forty yards when there was a terrible explosion. A Nebelwurfer is a German mortar that fires five three-inch mortars at a time. The mortar was the most feared of all weapons, and you could hear it in the distance. Those five hit right in the centre of my platoon. I went down, and when I looked around, I saw five or six guys crawling back toward the ditch. Thirteen of us were hit out of twenty-eight. A piece of shrapnel got me just behind the right knee. Much as I wanted to go on, I couldn't. I shouted at my two lead corporals to keep on going. Just then, our padre came along. I hate to tell this story. He was maybe twice my age, going on fifty, and three minutes after he saw my boys and saw what was happening on the beach, he was crying so hard I had to support him with my arm. It was a numbing experience.

I put the scabbard back onto my bayonet, so I could use the rifle as a crutch. I knew where the first-aid station would be. The surgeon cut my trouser legs and he said, "My God, you could go back to England." But I thought, Hell, I've done two years' training for this. I'm not going back. He put a dressing on my leg. It wasn't hurting so much. A truck came by with breaching equipment on it, and I crawled into the back, until we got to a little village. That's where I caught up with my troops. As I walked by a barn, I stopped for just a moment because here was a large white horse. Lying dead. But that wasn't what caught my attention. There was a little

An excerpt from Neily's log book listing the platoon members he led onto Sword Beach on June 6, 1944. Neily drew lines through the names of those wounded and killed during the operation.

blond boy. My first thought was, What's a blond boy doing in France? He was about four, maybe five years of age. He was lying right at the horse's head. And he was dead too. That will be with me forever.

For young, inexperienced soldiers, the road we were on the next day was pretty grim. It must have been a tough battle. There were many dead soldiers, both ours and the enemy's. Rifles with helmets hanging on them were stuck in the ground at the head of the bodies. I had never seen a dead person until the day before, and now there were dozens in the fields around us.

Later when our advance was halted we came across three more dead soldiers, two British and one enemy. We were not allowed to bury enemy soldiers, but we received permission to bury the two British. We placed their bodies in the graves. I had the men remove their helmets and, holding out the New Testament, somehow managed to recite the twenty-third Psalm, which came back to me from Sunday school. Sometime later, when no one seemed to be watching, I went over and repeated the same Psalm over the German. It seemed the thing to do.

In the few weeks that I was there, I was on the front lines the whole time. Sleep was a luxury. I don't believe I ever had more than two hours at a time. In late June, a large force of the enemy was dug in at the Château de La Londe. Mortars and machine-gun fire came from there almost every night. In the darkness, tracer bullets from machine-gun fire were frightening. Many farm animals had been killed, and the smell of dead animals was heavy in the air. We were given orders to attack at 4:30 in the morning on June 28. We were told there would be more guns than Montgomery had had at El Alamein. [See Glossary.]

The firing started on schedule. The noise was terrible. By the time we reached the row of trees along La Londe, it was dawn. I could see a stone wall maybe three hundred feet long. Tanks were approaching. I was checking on my unit, with my runner nearby, when a rifle shot rang out and he went down. A bullet through the head. The shot had come from the rear of the wall. With enemy tanks coming to our front and a sniper at our rear, we were in a bad position. I went with one of my most dependable men to eliminate the sniper. There was a small hole at the far end of the wall. I looked through, and there were the head and shoulders of a German with a rifle. I raised my rifle to fire. There was the immediate rip of a machine gun and I was hit. There was a terrific pain in my chest, and I had trouble breathing. The stretcher bearers found me and took me to a tank dugout. Fifteen wounded soldiers were already there. The orderly told me the bullet had gone through my chest, below my shoulder. He bandaged it well.

The sound of the tanks was now coming closer. At one point, bullets hit the turret above us and dirt began to fall on us. It was not a nice feeling. Then we saw a tank stop not a hundred feet away. It fired several times, and suddenly the tank commander came out of the turret and walked directly toward us, carrying a pistol. He was dressed as though he were on parade. Breeches with high leather boots. A four-inch cap. I thought to myself, By God, there's a gutsy bugger. He went straight to the edge of the dugout and stared down at us. I was trembling, but I didn't dare show it. He signalled us all to stand, and then swept the gun in the direction he had come. I took this to mean that we were to go to the German lines. I cautioned the men to do exactly as he indicated. He still had his gun and his tank. We proceeded for about eight hundred feet. There was much muttering and swearing. But gradually we moved away from the tank track to a wooded area off to the left. The tank commander was moving farther ahead into an orchard, and as we came closer to the trees, we were out of his line of vision and fire. A British officer suddenly appeared from the trees and signalled we were safe. Those who could, ran for it. The rest had to be helped.

After half an hour of walking, a jeep came along and they recognized my shoulder flashes. They were East Yorkies too. They took me to a field hospital. I was put to bed, dressed, and X-rayed. In addition to my serious chest wound, there were two long bullet grazes in my lower abdomen, with much blood. There was also blood on the left side of my face and my left eye was blinded. That lasted for about a month. When I recovered, I went to see the liaison officer to request an immediate return. And he said, "Well, I've just had a directive from Ottawa. No more CANLOAN officers who have been wounded should be sent back." The casualties had been 93 per cent.

When the war ended I was training with the gliders. We were to go to the Far East. In spite of everything I had been through, I wanted to go back. It's like being part of a hockey team. You're part of the team. You're needed.

Shoulder flashes for the East Yorkshire Battalion, including division and brigade.

"They started shelling one night,
and a shell went right down through
my jeep, through the driver's seat,
and never went off. If it had,
my bunker would still be going up."

WILLIAM NEWELL

WILLIAM NEWELL

I enlisted in London, Ontario, in May 1943. I was seventeen and a half. I signed up for the navy. The girls seemed to like navy uniforms better than the others. A little more excitement attached to it. Did it work? Oh, yes. Wonderful.

I did my basic training down in Cornwallis, Nova Scotia. Near the end of boot camp training, there were posters all over the place, asking for volunteers in different specialized services. The one I volunteered for was the RCN Beach Commando unit. Being young and a bit stupid, I wanted to get into the action. A few days later, I was foisted out of my barracks, put aboard a troop ship, and sent overseas. There were about ninety of us. We were the only Canadian commando unit in existence. The beach commandos didn't do raiding. We weren't hit-and-run. We were used where invasions took place. Beach commandos had the job of going in early and assessing what conditions were like on the beach, generally well ahead of the assault troops. Once the assault took place, it was our job to make sure the landing craft got cleared as quickly as possible in accordance with the tides. When a landing craft got hit, it was up to us to make sure it wasn't in

William Newell in his Royal Canadian Navy beach commando uniform, 1943.

Canadian Navy commandos training at a Scottish assault course in 1944.
Newell is in the background.

collision with an incoming craft. Essentially our job was to look after the movement of troops and mechanized equipment on the beach.

Our training was very specialized. There was so little time prior to the planned invasion of France that a training course lasted maybe ten days, not a lot of time to learn to operate a flame thrower or take apart a booby trap. We did sniper training, but mostly the focus was on heavy equipment and that's where it paid off. Had we not been well trained in that sort of thing, it would have been a complete disaster. There was a fair percentage of casualties in the training itself. Maybe 15 per cent. For example, we had to do baptism of fire so our obstacle course was done under live ammunition. Some of the fellows stood up at the wrong time and got hit. We'd also go through explosives that were set. When I questioned these things, I was simply told, Well, if you're going to get killed, we'd rather have it happen here than in combat. We had chemical-warfare training, where they sprayed mustard gas on you and you had to learn to get it off very quickly.

Off the roads, we had to ride Norton motorcycles, always standing up. I went over the handlebars about ten times. I was an expert at messing up motorcycles. Once, I had a bee in my helmet. I thought I had a B-17 in there. I was going along, banging on my helmet, and I went smack-bang into the biggest oak tree I could find. I bent the front wheel into an egg shape. I was half-dead, but it didn't really matter. We just made a joke of everything. Another time, we were on a convoy going along a road on Harley-Davidsons. About twenty of us. And the land army women were working in the fields. They would always wave at us, and the chap ahead of me was going along waving back and ran right into a parked car. He and the bike both went over the car. His bike was a wreck and he was stagger-ing around, trying to get up. I couldn't stop laughing. I said to him, "Well, you won't keep your eyes off the girls." Typical Canadian, I guess. The more desperate things got, the funnier things became.

We didn't go into France until a few days after D-Day. We relieved another commando unit. It was frustrating being held back. We were ready. It was sort of like standing on the edge of a diving board, ready to go over. It was just as well for us, but still. We landed on Juno Beach, Mike Red sector. We could see the shellfire. We could see the smoke and hear the explosions. They had very large battleships lying off of us, six or seven miles, and they were firing over the beach at the Germans. It was mostly logistical stuff we did. But it was tough working there. People were still being killed on the beach. The Germans were uncanny with their 88s. They were also shelling from St.-Lo, more than twenty miles away. It was a 200 mm railway gun. Tremendously precise. If their shells exploded on impact, you could drop two or three houses in the crater. Occasionally the shell wouldn't go off. I had a jeep and parked it outside my bunker. They started shelling one night, and a shell went right down through my jeep, through the driver's seat, and never went off. If it had, my bunker would still be going up.

You had to find your own place to bunk down and call home. The Germans had a very complex tunnel system through there. I went into one of their bunkers for shelter, and it was where they had slept. It was only about four feet high, but, gosh, it had a big bed. There were sixteen army blankets on it. There was a pile of sandbags from the earth to the ceiling. Pinned to one of the sandbags was a picture of Betty Grable taking a milk bath, if you can believe that. Obviously the enemy appreciated the same things we did.

There's another incident I really remember well. There was quite a stream of vehicles coming to the beach carrying casualties and POWs to be put on ships to take them to England. One young German, he was in the Panzer group, had his left arm off just below the shoulder. He still had a miserable field dressing on it, but he wouldn't accept any help jumping down from the truck. He landed in front of me and, of course, he fell. I reached down to help him, but he shook me off. He stood up very close to me and stared into my eyes. I don't think I ever saw hatred like that. And he spit in my face. I heard him say, "Schwein!" ["Pig!"] And he turned around and walked up the ramp with his field dressing dripping. My first impulse was to shoot him, and I almost did. It was just naked hatred. But I lowered my weapon and turned around. I was stunned. I just shook my head and said, "What kind of a war is this?" It's stuck in my mind for a long time.

I got wounded during the shelling. On the LCTs, they had very big grates on the ramps. They were very heavy to take the weight of the tanks. I got knocked down by a shell, concussed, and my legs went through the ramp. It was at night. I was scared silly that the next tank was going to come down and run over me. That had happened to a friend of mine two nights before. But my buddy who was with me managed to get me out. I couldn't walk. There was no shrapnel wound, but it had torn the heck out of the joint. Fortunately, they had a MASH hospital just up over the hill. I thought it was painful until I got to that hospital and I thought, My God. I was in the corner of a forty-bed ward. A young lad was in the bed beside me. He was seventeen. He had his right leg off. The fellow on my other side had both hands off. Those were the kind of things you ran into in the hospital. The young lads with the shock in their eyes. There was no fun there. I certainly had to admire the dedication of the medical people. For the most part, they did surgery right in the wards. The beds were quite close. That hospital is where all my maturing took place. It was a very traumatic experience. That was the other side of the glory.

The exciting part was flying over the invasion back to England on a nice sunny morning, seeing the entire thing from the air. Five thousand ships. It was an unforgettable sight. My wound healed quickly and I was soon back on my feet. I left my crutches at the hospital, but I used a cane. They sent me right back. There was a lot of that. They couldn't get qualified replacements. That's why they started conscription. My friend Walter had been hit rather hard through the neck. He shouldn't have been sent back, but he was, and he was killed by a sniper.

It took two days to cross the English Channel because we were shepherding some old trawlers that were full of ammunition. When we got off at Arromanches, they threw out the anchor. The captain wouldn't take me in. He said I could swim the rest of the way, if I wanted to. But the cook said, "We've got a little eight-foot dory here. I'm going to row you in." So I made my second landing on Normandy in a rowboat. He supplied me with a two-quart bottle of rum. He said that would see me through. How we didn't get run over by landing craft I have no idea. I gave him a push off from the beach, and that was the last I saw of him.

That was on Sword Beach. I had to hitchhike up to Juno. When I got there, my unit had moved. No one had any idea where they'd gone. I spent a couple of days in behind Gold Beach operating tanks. I finally found my unit and helped finish up clearing the beach. Then the brass decided, for reasons best known to themselves, not to make use of a highly trained unit such as ourselves on further invasion work up the coast. Even though good replacements were much in demand, they sent us back to Canada. We had a funny group of officers. Prior to going over the first time, one of them jumped out of a second-storey building and broke both ankles so he wouldn't have to go. There were some strange things going on.

Newell (second from the left) and others with G.I. Jill, a wartime entertainer, at the Hollywood, California, "Brown Derby" restaurant in September 1945.

When we got back to Stadacona in Halifax, we were immediately told in the drill hall, "Get those damned khaki uniforms off. You're in the navy." It was a terrible, demoralizing thing. It was so bad that my buddy deserted. He just never came back. He went home, then went north in the woods and hid. Meanwhile, I was put on the naval police force. One day I was assigned to Union Station to pick up some prisoners. My buddy was one of them. I was also given the pleasure of escorting him to his court martial. He got a dishonourable discharge and six months hard labour. And you know, the guy was a good man. That's how the navy worked. I could have shot half the guys in charge and been quite happy doing it.

I went through the Halifax Riots at the end of the war. Halifax was anticipating a big celebration, because there were something like forty thousand sailors there. So everyone was afraid of a big rough party, I guess. About a week before, they began boarding up restaurants and the liquor and beer stores. They boarded everything up. Barrington Street was vacant. This was the wrong thing to do. When the ships came in, the sailors were given leave and they just ganged up. First they broke into a beer store, then they took five liquor stores. Three fellows were killed in the riots. They found one of them outside my bedroom window, out in Dalhousie. They finally imposed martial law after three days. It was quite an experience.

I should also mention the flag. We were unloading an LCC on the beach one time and the landing craft got hit. It was sinking and the high tide was coming in. We managed to get the tanks off. Then, when I looked back, just at dusk, I could see this poor old White Ensign trying to fly on the jack staff. The crew had left, but I made my way back on board and I took what was left of the White Ensign and stuffed it in my battle tunic. Why did I do it? You might think, Who cared? But we didn't have that attitude in our training. The flag was uppermost. The be-all and the end-all. That's what we were there for. So when I went back and got that flag, it was out of natural instinct. I was just not going to let the flag go down with the boat. I still have it. I've never done a thing to it. It was full of smoke, full of holes. I've never washed it. It has always been a symbol to me.

"When you get hit, you know you're hit.
I was stunned. I didn't feel the pain
because my adrenalin was going at
two thousand and four per cent."

T. GARRY GOULD

T. GARRY GOULD

I was born in Montreal in June 1922. I was an NDG [Notre-Dame-de-Grâce] boy. I enlisted in July 1942. We were three boys in the family. After we all joined, my mother's hair went white. This fellow Hershey and I were to be sent to Dundurn, Saskatchewan, for basic training. But neither of us wanted to be anything other than in great big tanks, and we were allowed to go to Camp Borden and then to Gordon Head to train in major tanks. Gordon Head was officer training. One day we were supposed to learn how to address the troop. I'd studied some pamphlets the night before. So I stood up in front of the boys and I said, "Okay now, men. You must realize that war is hell." Of course my expressions were a little bit youthful or something, and my friend Kirk Cole, a red-haired fellow from Toronto, was rolling on the ground laughing at me. He just couldn't hold it in any longer. In the fullness of time, a German 88 took Kirk's head right off. So I don't have a lot of fun telling this story, but . . . I don't say stupid, I don't say innocent . . . we were what we were. We were trying to be mature. I didn't smoke, drink, or run around. I took the other attitude. I had my nose to the grindstone. I was serious about trying to do my best.

T. Garry Gould, commander of "A" Squadron Sherbrooke Fusilier Regiment.

We were loaded on trains at Camp Borden on August 13, Friday the 13th, to take us for embarkation in Halifax. My father knew which train I was on and he watched it go by. He already had one son doing the Boston-Newfie run and here was his second son going overseas. Within a couple of hours of landing, we were on a train to Aldershot. General List. We weren't part of a regiment, which meant we couldn't go anywhere. We all would have died to have a regimental affiliation, because it meant you had arrived. With General List, you can have a cup of tea by yourself, because nobody wants you. It was a very awkward feeling.

But lo and behold, about seven o'clock one night, they put us aboard some landing craft infantry and tossed us across the English Channel. It was one week after D-Day when we landed on Juno Beach. It looked like there'd been two thousand train wrecks. It was a big mess. We were delivering tanks and we were under fire. We were kicking up some dust so their artillery could easily find us. But I didn't stop what I was doing. I'd go down a row of tanks and I'd recite the twenty-third Psalm: "Though I walk through the valley of the shadow of death, I will fear no evil."

Two weeks after we'd arrived, we were bivouacked north of Caen, and we got an urgent call at night from the Sherbrooke Fusiliers for five officers down at Lebisey Wood. When we got there, some of the vehicles were still smouldering. The medics had gone with the wounded. The killed had been taken care of. The adjutant had had quite a day. He just said, "Crawl under the nearest tank and we'll see you in the morning." Our boys were very good at liberating bottles of Calvados from the basements of houses. That's how I met my regiment. Everyone was enjoying a drink. The casualty rate for the regiment was around 50 per cent. For junior officers, it was probably 250 per cent. That's why I was given lots of training

The insignia of the Sherbrooke Fusilier regiment, which was formed from two sister regiments in Sherbrooke for wartime service. In 1942 the regiment became an armoured field unit.

and lots of inspiration. You have to stick your neck out as a junior officer. End of sermon.

The Sherman was an excellent tank. Numbers outlast perfection. The Germans and the Russians went for bigger tanks, but they didn't have to put them on trains, load them in holds, and ship them across the North Atlantic. They didn't have to put them on landing craft tanks and send them across the Channel. Most Sherman tanks had a 75 mm gun, and that was close to being equal with the 88, which was the feared German gun on their tanks. I never looked back once I made the decision to join tanks. With the Sherman tank, you were mobile over any ground. They had lots of ammunition. There was fuel available and a good radio set. They had a generator to charge up the batteries. Our clothes and kit were stacked on the rear deck. We weren't being picked off by small-arms fire. We weren't stepping on mines. We could be pretty supportive of the infantry, and shoot into buildings and towns. It was the best place to be. It was the most commanding. We set the pace of the war. We got the job done. A lot of times, we got the enemy to turn and take off. But if the shells came in and blasted you, it was game over, often within a millisecond, because we were carrying forty-two rounds, as well as small arms and grenades. I've been beside tanks that went clunk, bang, and then silence. It's over so quick.

I was in the attack in the operation called Totalise. We lined up at Verrieres Ridge, the night of August 7 and 8. There were one million soldiers. The infantry were in protected vehicles called kangaroos. We were in our tanks, leading. Artillery was covering the flanks and the ground ahead. At eleven o'clock sharp, the command was given to advance. We weren't firing. I was absolutely amazed. I had been sitting on top of the turret because I was trying to show that there was nothing to fear. My sergeant's face, when he led the first part of the attack, was white as a sheet. I could see it from the artificial moonlight we got by putting searchlights on the low clouds. I decided to go ahead with my troop and lead the regiment. No one else was forward of me. There were a million people behind me. Ahead of me, all I could see were open fields, some copse, bushes, and orchards. Just steady speed, so we all stay together. But the Germans knew we were coming.

At first light, we were on target, and the Germans were firing at us because we had stopped. The brigadier went to a spot no one else would go to because it didn't supply enough cover. As he was crawling out of his turret, he got plugged. I was new to the battle at large, and I was trying to do what was right, so I decided to pull out of the line, go forward, and investigate. I pulled out and spotted a whole lot of Wehrmacht, which is the German infantry conscript guys, in the orchard, in the grass. We couldn't go in there very easily with tanks, so I stayed out of the orchard. I had all my guns firing. They were firing at me pretty good. I had about five minutes with them, and they weren't about to surrender, and I wasn't about to let them take care of our guys. They'd already nicked the brigadier.

Meanwhile, I heard the colonel call the squadron leader because four enemy tanks were coming up the road. He called for a troop to be sent in. It wasn't me because they saw I was engaged. I don't know how many troops were sent, but we were not going to back up this time. This was the breakout. And this was it for [Michael] Whitman, the German tank ace. With his skill, he had personally, in his own tank, knocked off more than 130 units on the Eastern Front. So it was a major deal. I think it's generally accepted that the Canadian tanks got him. If I hadn't been picking off the infantry, maybe I'd have been up there. The troop leader who succeeded in stopping Whitman lasted only another four days. I just missed going up against him. But that's war. You can't choose.

I was waist out of the turret, firing that machine gun, moving the tank all the time, which I guess prevented them from knocking my head off. But I got plugged in the shoulder and I dropped. When you get hit, you know you're hit. I was stunned. I didn't feel the pain because my adrenalin was going at two thousand and four per cent. You know you're in trouble, you know you've lost your effectiveness, and you're embarrassed because you've blundered. The medics came to pick me up. I was twice knocked out on the operating table, but they couldn't get the bullet out. It's still in my shoulder. After a few days, the medics said goodbye to me, because we were short of people at the front. They wanted you back in the line.

Waiting for the "Blockbuster" on a night push toward Goch
on the Siegfried Line, February 7-8, 1945.

In one attack in Belgium, the Germans had knocked out three tanks
and the boys in the fourth tank had jumped out. I was then a squadron
leader. When I got up there, I saw one of our guys lying down, dead, facing
a burning tank. Sergeant Ames was in pain. The rest of the boys were
dead. I'd already lost four tanks and, bingo, we start to lose another four,
another troop. Only one tank was left undamaged. It was a straight road.

No way off. The Germans could pick us off at a quarter-mile away. But the colonel caught up with us, and he drove home a lesson that night I'll never forget. He rammed his finger into my breastbone hard enough to bruise it. "Don't you ever back up. If you're taking casualties and you're getting discouraged, don't ever back up. You will take more casualties backing up and somebody else is going to have to go in after you to take up that position again, and there will still be more casualties. So keep going."

In the winter of 1945, I was out in front, south of Niemagen, facing the Siegfried Line. The war slowed down a little because it was so darn cold and miserable. Then it was breakout time again. We had to go through the Siegfried Line. So eleven o'clock at night, we were all lined up. Then we started to inch forward and we hit mines. I had to plan to get around the minefield in the dark. I issued orders that were successful, but some of the boys lost their lives. We got on target. I was on top of the infantry colonel's tank when there was an explosion. I think it was a mortar. It flung me unconscious. It killed the colonel, who was in his infantry kangaroo. It must have hit the top of the deck, blown me off, and got him. When I came to, I saw Jim Love, the gunner, and my crew coming toward me. But the Germans were waiting for targets, and one of the crew, David, got killed. Now, I have to tell you that when I was just a new squadron leader, David was on guard duty one night. It was getting cold and he went unconscious. He was discovered and paraded in before me by a couple of sergeants. They were looking at me and I didn't know what to do. So I pounded the table and said, "Guilty." But that didn't seem to be enough. There had to be a punishment. So then I said, "Confined to barracks for twenty-four hours." That seemed to satisfy them, and off they went. I don't know where the inspiration came from. There was nowhere for him to go anyway, so it was really nothing. And that was the lad who was killed trying to help me. At the time, I had to say something. The fact that the sergeant seemed happy with the punishment made me feel that I'd done all right. Then to see him lose his life. Oh boy. These things never leave you.

But we were on target. We'd followed the colonel's dictum of never backing up. We got the job done. That's why I was recognized after getting

Courtesy Montreal Gazette

Gould reunites with his family (including his two brothers who served in the navy
and air force) at the Bonaventure railway station in Montreal. Gould is in the centre.

out of the hospital. They trotted me off to see King George, and he pinned
a military cross on my chest. There are no medals in the Canadian Army
or any other army when you don't succeed, even though you take a terrible
beating. Napoleon figured this out years ago: people will give their lives
for a one-inch medal pinned on their chest.

They evacuated me by air for England. There was a fair amount of
metal in me: In the backside, the back, the legs. One arm broken. One
hand in pieces. I had been knocked unconscious and had back strain. I
had to wear a support for years. I was in hospital there for five months.
One time I woke up screaming because I saw this horde of German
uniforms coming at me, and there was no way I could stop them. The fear
and trauma finally caught up with me. I came home on a hospital ship in
July 1945. The war was something I wanted to do. I hope I did it well. I had
my Bible all the way through and the regimental badge. That's something
you don't dishonour.

"I was blown out of the carrier fifteen
yards up the road. The last thing
I remember was just a gentle puff,
a little zephyr of wind, on the
side of my face and I was gone."

REX FENDICK

REX FENDICK

I had hoped to become a machine-gun officer. That requires a lot of specialist training and I got accepted. I went to the machine-gun wing at the Brockville Officer Training Centre and then the Canadian Machine Gun Training Centre at Three Rivers, Quebec. By January 1943, I was still only eighteen years old, so I was taken off the overseas draft and sent back to the Saint John Fusiliers. But that night I was ordered on a train and ended up in Nanaimo, British Columbia. We went through Vancouver on a bright, sunny day in January. The ladies were out walking around in summer dresses and we still had on all our winter kit – fur hats, mitts, overshoes. Later, they sent our battalion by road to Prince George. It was deep winter and the Fraser Canyon Highway in those days was a lot different than it is now. Only one vehicle wide, chiselled right out of the rock. The water coming out of the rocks would run right across the road and freeze and form an outward sloping ice sheet. No guardrails. We took seven days to do the five hundred miles. We didn't have any casualties, but they sent a brigade up on the road behind us and they lost several men. They just went over the side.

Rex Fendick at eighteen years of age upon being commissioned as a Canadian Army officer with the Saint John Fusiliers.

While we were in Prince George, word came from Ottawa about the CANLOAN scheme. They were calling for volunteers to go into the British army. Six of us from the Fusiliers volunteered. I was fed up being in Canada. I'd joined up to go overseas and fight in the war, and it didn't look like it was going to happen. And I was with a zombie unit that wasn't going anywhere. I jumped at the chance. We sailed in May 1944 and first went to a Scottish division. But we were all trained machine gunners and felt we were being wasted. It was obvious D-Day was very close because they were waterproofing their vehicles. We asked if we could be sent to machine-gun units, so they sent us all to a reinforcement holding unit. We went to Normandy on D-plus-nine. There was still some sporadic fire coming in on the beach, but nothing so you'd notice. We landed at one of the docks that ran out maybe three hundred yards from shore. It was just a single strand of floating steel pontoons. We stepped off the ramp of our landing craft onto the steel pontoons, got our boots wet, and walked ashore.

We were only half a mile inland and at night it was sheer murder. The anti-aircraft fire was going up so thick pilots could have walked on it. All the ships and the ack-ack on shore were firing. And it was coming back down, of course. We had no shovels. No way to dig in. We just lay there under a tree and the stuff would be slashing down, chopping branches off the tree. I still have my old sleeping bag with a hole in it where one piece went through. One morning, Mac McConaghy, who was my chum from the Fusiliers, came over and said, "They're looking for two officers for the Middlesex Regiment. Shall we go?" I said, "Why not?" We reported to the CO and rode motorbikes up to a place called Cam's Wood, which had been counter-attacked heavily a half-hour before we got there. There had been merciless shelling and mortaring. They were still gathering up casualties and burying them. That was my baptism of fire. My machine-gun platoon was in action that night.

We were part of Operation Goodwood in Normandy. That was the biggest chance we had to fire directly on the enemy. We went up on the ridge, flanking the flat plain where the tanks went south, past the city of Caen. Our troops were at the edge of a wood that surrounded a wheat field. At the other end of the field, four hundred yards away, was a French château. The Germans were just swarming around that château. We started firing at it as soon as we got there. There was also a barn in the wheat field about three hundred yards away that I knew would be occupied. So I put all the guns on the barn. Shot the devil out of it. I told the fellows to hit the eave line and the floor line where they would be. Immediately a dozen Germans came racing out of the barn. I was looking at the troops through my binoculars when I saw a German officer standing with his binoculars, looking at me! I let my binoculars drop and about fifty yards away a big German helmet popped up. I immediately put a couple of guns right on the wheat. We chewed that up pretty thoroughly. He either got his head down and crawled away, or he was hit. We were mortared steadily the whole night. We didn't get hit, but in the morning we buried three hundred men up there. That was heavy.

After the city of Caen was captured, the whole division was moved to the extreme right of the British Second Army. The first place we went into was called Monty's Hangar. It was a very deep, broad valley. We were on one side and Jerry was on the other side. They had mined that whole slope. A divisional attack was successful, and I led the company up to consolidate. I took the lead vehicle. We crossed a little scissors bridge, a couple of fields, and then up a lane past a château. These things stick with you. I made a left turn in the lane, and we hit a mine. My driver was killed outright. He was cut off at the waist. I was blown out of the carrier fifteen yards up the road. The last thing I remember was just a gentle puff, a little zephyr of wind, on the side of my face and I was gone. I sailed through the air. I came to in the regimental aid post.

I got a mixture of sand and gravel splinters in my legs and one eardrum was perforated. We went by motor ambulance to a British field hospital. I was in the front seat with the driver. I saw red flashing lights coming toward us. There were two motorcycles and a big open car. Monty [General Montgomery] was in it. And he saluted *me*. But I couldn't return the salute because I didn't have a hat on. I'd lost it. I spent about ten days in hospital. They didn't try to pick any of the bits and pieces out of me. They left them in. For ten years afterwards, the splinters kept popping out

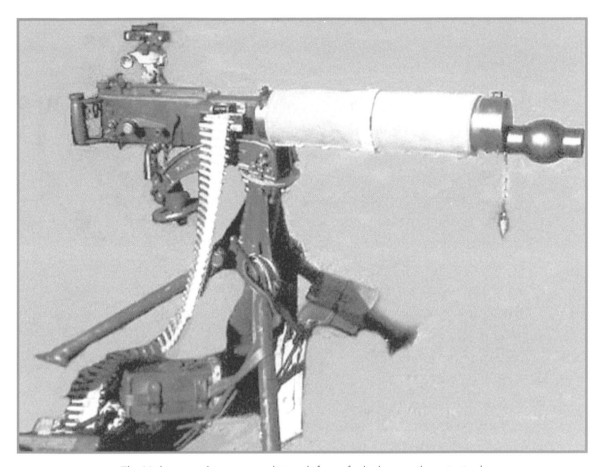

The Vickers machine gun and tripod, four of which were the principal weapons of the machine-gun platoon commanded by Fendick.

spontaneously. From the hospital, I went back to the unit and took over my platoon again.

There were four Vickers machine guns in the platoon. The Vickers gun was used for both direct and indirect fire. You either engaged targets you could see through the sights, or you laid it like an artillery piece by instruments and fired at unseen targets. There was a lot of geometry involved. The deeper you got into it, the more engrossed you became. You'll never find a fellow trained on a Vickers machine gun who didn't love it. I directed the fire. Each gun had a dial sight, mounted on the side of the gun, that could lay off horizontal angles. It had a vertical adjustment for elevation and levelling bubbles. I could direct the guns onto a target that we couldn't see. We had a maximum range of forty-five hundred yards. The guns were quite effective. If you selected your position carefully and the range was relatively long, the trajectory of the ammunition would be falling fairly steeply by the time the ammunition reached the end of its life. It would go down into the slit trenches. Another job we did a lot was called harassing fire. We would blanket an area with continuous fire and deny its use to the enemy.

Any time we fired, we were very much a target. The Germans excelled at sound location. They would quickly pick up a machine gun firing. If we were firing for three or four minutes, we knew we were going to be hit before we got out of there. We'd keep moving. Shoot and scoot. When we couldn't move, we just hunkered down and took it. If we were in a defensive position where we knew we were going to have to stay, the first thing we did was dig in. If we got down into a well-built slit trench, our odds were pretty good.

We motored all the way up to the Meuse-Escaut Canal between Belgium and Holland. That was an assault crossing. Quite a sticky one. The machine guns fired to support the assault across the river. Then the engineers constructed a bridge and we drove across. We ended up at a place called Cuyk, a little village on the Maas River. That was a very nasty period. We had bad weather, very bad. It was getting into November. It was boggy country. The ground was all marsh. It was open in a lot of places. No cover. You couldn't dig in effectively. It was heavily mined and the Germans had perfect observations for long distances. They could tell where we were and mortar us at will.

We first took a town called Overloon. That was a very stiff battle. It took our whole division three or four days. Our guys were miserable. The conditions were terrible. Cold. Muddy. Lots of shellfire. You get very tired and you stay very tired. You're never in top form. But the attitude was: Let's get on with it. We kicked off for the next town just ten clicks [kilometres] away. It took us seven days. It was absolute misery. Mud, wet, cold, mine shells, mortars, machine guns, you name it. The frost wasn't enough to freeze the ground, so we were always breaking into mud. We were moving continually, jumping from one spot to another, jiggering around all the time. In those seven days, the longest time we ever spent in one place was maybe a few hours.

It was at night when we got to the Rhine. We went into one farm there, set up our guns, and laid them across the river into the German city of Rees, directly opposite us. We didn't think much about it being Germany. We'd been firing on towns, cities, everything. It was just another target. The next morning we saw the big Royal Navy launches, which they brought up to take Churchill, Eisenhower, and General Allenbrook across the river. Rees was totally flattened. Just smashed. We fired steadily for thirty-six hours. That was the longest we ever did. We had an army service corps platoon carrying ammunition up to us. We had cooks, drivers, clerks, anyone who could walk take shifts on the guns. We were laying down a solid belt of fire across the northern flank of the bridgehead trying to prevent the Germans from coming down to attack from the north.

The bridge was built at Rees very quickly. A pontoon bridge. We crossed that, swung north back into a corner of Holland and then into Germany again. We weren't allowed to associate with any of the Germans. The lid was clamped down tight. They were the enemy. We went into one farm. There was a little girl there, ten or twelve years old. I got her to do some laundry for me. I had a hard time getting her to accept a bar of chocolate for doing it. That was the atmosphere. The German people were very frightened and suspicious. We couldn't trust them because we didn't know who they were. So we kept our distance. For a long time, we didn't trust anybody.

One time, the Germans had us surrounded in this village. We had several fights there. I got up in the top of a three-storey building on the village square, and the tank down below fired and knocked a corner off the building. It didn't collapse, so we were all right. I celebrated my twenty-first birthday there. I wrote a letter to my dad and said, "Today, I am a man."

As we moved up through Germany, we began to see all kinds of refugees on the road. There were a lot of concentration camp uniforms mixed in with them. The first camp to be liberated was in our sector. Belsen. I always remember when our CO came back and told us about it.

He'd seen Belsen. Been in it. He was just livid. He was almost speechless. It was unbelievable. They wouldn't let the troops go into those places, so I didn't see it myself. But we did see a lot of concentration camp survivors wandering the roads in their black-and-white-striped uniforms with the little pillbox hat. It's the saddest memory I have of the way the Germans treated people.

"I was fortunate to have landed in a ploughed-up field. I buried my chute. I was fine. Luck was with me, and luck was with me for thirteen months of evasion."

MICHAEL FEDORUK

MICHAEL FEDORUK

I joined up with the air force in Edmonton in 1942. I was twenty-one. I was athletically inclined and I figured I could be a good pilot. Then I found out during training in Saskatoon that there were too many young aircrew better suited than I was. So I decided to go in as a bomb aimer. I was disappointed, but I took to it. I was keen. I got to be up front, still staying in aircrew and going operational. You betcha.

I hit England in 1943. I was with the RAF, the 44 Rhodesian Squadron based out of Lincoln. Our logo was an elephant's head. It was a very good squadron, but it flew a lot of missions and a lot of aircraft got shot down. It's kind of hard to explain how we kept going. You just went along with the crowd. You don't want to be a coward. You figured you're going to make the grade, eh, and come out alive.

We'd take off in the evenings. Usually our trips were seven to eight hours long. We'd get back about four o'clock in the morning, just as dawn was breaking. We had Lincoln Cathedral as a good landmark. We'd have coffee and get debriefed about what we saw, how many planes we saw, etc.

Michael Fedoruk, a flight sergeant with the Royal Canadian Air Force, in dress uniform when he enlisted in 1942.

Fedoruk (kneeling, on the right) with Lancaster Bomber Command Group 5 RAF crew after a trip debriefing, warming up to a hot stove and a cup of tea, February 1944.

We carried one four-thousand pounder, a two-tonner. We called that the Blockbuster. We also carried twenty-five or so fragmentation bombs and the rest were incendiaries, crates of them. Four-pound sticks, about sixteen inches long, about two inches in diameter. They were supposed to be dropped in the area of the Blockbuster and start fires. We were sent out to demoralize, damage, splinter, and fire. Pathfinder planes would go out ahead of us and they'd drop incendiaries – green, blue, or red markers in the target area. We could hear them on the intercom, "Bomb the cluster of green markers." Well, I'd be down in my bombsight, looking out ahead. I'd be directing the pilot, giving him corrections. The bomb doors would be opened by the pilot. I'd sight the target area and when it was ready I'd push the bomb release button and drop the load. You could feel the plane lurch up a little. And I'd tell the pilot, "Bombs are gone. Bombs away. It's your baby, now." It took quite a while for the bombs to get down there. I thought I was a good bomb aimer. In those days, factories were important. Railways were important. But because of the way the Germans were bombing our cities, the RAF figured, Well, we might as well destroy Berlin and let's do it. That was Bomber Harris. [See Glossary.]

My memories of that night are still vivid. It was about two hours past midnight on a cloudless night, March 25, 1944. We'd unleashed approximately 9,360 pounds of destruction on our target in Berlin less than half an hour earlier. We were scooting back to Great Britain and safety. Then I realized that a grave navigational error had been made and we were going over the Ruhr Valley, a heavily defended area. I wasn't with my usual crew. My skipper was sick, so I'd volunteered to take the place of another crew's bomb aimer who was also sick. The navigator piped up and said, "Hey, I think you're right, Mike. The winds have changed. We're a little off track." Just ahead of us, I saw a Lancaster blow up. And then we got coned. It was not a nice feeling. There were flak bursts above us, below us, and to the side. At the same time, the pilot was doing evasive action. Corkscrewing left and right. Diving. We finally got out of the searchlight and the pilot said, "We've made it." I looked down and saw tracers from below coming up at our aircraft.

A night fighter got us from below. Those night fighters had cannons pointing upwards and when they found you, all they had to do was fly below you, rake your wingtips, set you on fire, and then take off. We got hit on the left wing, both motors, and we were on fire. The skipper, he was cursing, struggling, and sweating. "I can't hold it any longer, fellas. Let's start bailing out." It was do or die. I said to the rest of the crew, "Okay, I'm going to leave," hoping they'd follow. I was lying right on top of the escape hatch, so it was a piece of cake. My chute opened. I was dangling and looking up, and I couldn't see any other chutes. I couldn't see the plane either.

Much later on, I got a letter from a fellow who was doing research on planes that crashed in Holland. And this letter came to me literally fifty years to the day that I was shot down. One of his projects was to find out what happened to the plane that I was in, ME672. He had remembered his father saying, "Let's go see this burning plane." My plane had crashed in a wood, just short of a lake, and the Germans were still there, retrieving the

No.44 (Rhodesia) Squadron,
R.A.F. Station,
Dunholme Lodge,
Lincoln.

25th March, 1944.

Dear Mr Fedoruk,

It is with deep regret that I have to confirm the news that your son Flight Sergeant Michailo Fedoruk failed to return from an operational flight over enemy ————— on the night of 24/25th March, 1944. May I, on behalf of the Squadron, take this opportunity of expressing our most profound sympathy to you in your anxiety, and we all sincerely hope that he is safe and well as a prisoner of war.

The procedure for transmitting names of prisoners of war to this country is rather slow, and it may be several weeks before information of this nature regarding your son reaches me, but as soon as any such news is forthcoming you may be sure I will inform you immediately by cable.

Your son has been serving with the Squadron since 19th February, 1944, during which period he has shown himself to be a very keen and reliable Air Bomber, carrying out all his duties with great skill and determination.

Yours Sincerely
S.L. Cockbain /s/c

S. L. COCKBAIN,
Commanding,
No.44 (Rhodesian) Squadron.

T. Fedoruk Esq.,
954 - 104 Avenue,

A letter to Fedoruk's parents from his commanding officer informing them that their son was declared missing in action in an operation flight over Berlin, March 25, 1944.

dead bodies. I figured the pilot must have been trying to make it to the lake. When he'd hit the trees, he must have catapulted, because the rear gunner's turret landed in the lake about a hundred yards away. The Germans had just removed the turret out of the lake and he was still inside. This was all a shock to me, and the first inkling I had as to what actually happened to my plane. All I knew was that my crew members were dead and I was the sole survivor.

I was fortunate to have landed in a ploughed-up field. I buried my chute. I was fine. Luck was with me, and luck was with me for thirteen months of evasion. I knew I was in Holland. I travelled for three or four days and I came to this farmyard. Out came a young fellow who could speak English. He was hiding out at his parents' farm because he had to report to the Germans for work. He was just as scared as I was. Several days later, he showed up with a friend from the Dutch underground. I got suited up in civilian clothes and we took off. First stop was a little village pub. He ordered beers. He was talking to me in English. I said, "Isn't it

Fedoruk (second from the right) and two other evading airmen are given
a farewell tea party by the Ottens family in Amersfoort, Holland,
before being escorted to their next destination by the underground, April 1944.

kind of dangerous to be speaking to me in English?" And he said, "Naw, they're just a bunch of dumb Dutchmen. All they know is Dutch. They won't bother us." Later, we came to this residence where they produced passports for downed flyers. We took the train to Amersfoort, up north. Just before we got there, the train stopped and the Gestapo came on board, checking passports. And I thought, Uh oh. These two guards were just three feet away from me when the train stopped and people made a mad dash to get off. My contact motioned me to get off too. I dodged the two guards and got off the train and onto the platform. Just like that. Another close call.

Our next stop in Amersfoort was at the house of a Dutch policeman. My American friend, Chuck, a flyer I met earlier with the underground, was there too. We stayed for two weeks because a bunch of key personnel in the underground were caught. The escape route had to be re-established. Every evening, this Dutch policeman would bring out his hidden radio and we'd listen to the BBC news. The Dutch people were incredibly brave. This guy had three daughters – aged two, three, and five – and he stuck his neck out. With a family like that, eh.

We were then moved to a farm. The farmer had twelve kids, and six of us airmen boarded at his place. We plucked weeds. We hoed. We made hay.

We kept ourselves busy. We slept in the haylofts. Three Dutch people were hiding there as well. But there were too many of us and it was getting to be too big a strain on the farmer. So Chuck and I were transferred to Nijverdal. We boarded with a safe house. He was a druggist. And Chucky, he got in trouble with a young girl there. He started to get too friendly with her. One day, the father came up and saw Chucky and her playfully pushing each other around. And he said, "Hey, hey. That's it." We had to move. We moved into the countryside about eight kilometres out of town. A week later we heard that we had just missed a raid by the Gestapo on the safe house. So it was a good thing that Chucky had horsed around.

I spent seven months at the country place. The family worked in a factory in Nijverdal. I stayed at home. Chuck decided to go on his own to try to get to the Allied lines. He asked me to come along and I said, "Good God, no. You'll never make it." Mind you, the invasion was on and the armies were coming up. I heard later that he made it back to the place where we got our passports. The Dutch underground was furious that I had let Chuck go. They said that if I tried the same stunt, they would have to shoot me, because it would put too many people in jeopardy. I promised I would stay put. The family I stayed with were good people: Geritt, a young boy my age, Dinka, a young girl about five years older, and the parents. We really got along. The mother called me son and I called her mother. I got pretty fluent in Dutch. I was there seven months – that's a long time. I'd go for walks in the evening. I'd whittle Plexiglas into ornaments, or whittle out chess pieces.

One night the girl and I went out for a walk and along came a German on a bicycle. He caught us off guard. It was after curfew. He stopped and said, "How late is it?" I understood what he said so I looked at my watch and said, "Quarter to ten." And he says, "Danke schon," and away he went. They weren't looking for escapees. He was just looking for the time. That was it. Another close call.

You lost your fear on the run, but every place you stayed, you slept with your clothes beside you in case you had to make a fast move. You always had an escape route and a place to hide. We did get caught at the country home by a surprise raid in the area. The mother woke up and started screaming. The Germans were all the way down the road. There were four of us staying in the house at that time. We went directly to our hideout underneath the stairs. There was a soldier out front and Dinka figured, Well, I've got to soften him up somehow. She asked him if he'd like a cup of coffee. He said sure. She brought him out some imitation coffee and a cookie. He thanked her and left us alone. He never came in the house and there we were hiding under the stairs.

This young British fella staying with me was moved to another home in the area, and by God, wouldn't you know it, he got caught there. He was staying with another young boy. They got caught and put in jail. When they were being escorted to some other place, they were both shot. They were just left in the bush. There was another close call that I had.

In the meantime, the armies were slowly coming toward my location. I was hoping that I could beat the odds and come out of it alive, and I did. One of the neighbours came by and said, "They're here." The Canadian Army was in Nijverdal. I came up to an army guy cooking some water on a little butane stove. They wanted to debrief me right away, so there was just no way of giving the family I stayed with a proper goodbye. I gave Geritt a hug and thank you, and then he knew I had to go.

In a few days, I was transported back to England. The family never talked about why they were risking their lives for us. I think they were just being friendly to people who were trying to free them. They got money and ration coupons from the underground. In return, they kept us hidden. I always said to myself, I could never repay those people for the good they did me. I wish I'd had the bucks to do it. But you just can't re-pay kindness like that. I figured maybe the army and the air force would repay them a little bit. Because they suffered an awful lot. Food in Nijverdal was very, very scarce. They had a terrible time. I was just skin and bones. When I got back to England, I went to a warehouse where the parcels sent to me were stored. I had smokes. I had jam, jellies, fruits, canned goods, everything. My kid brother was in Holland and he came to England to visit me. We spent VE day together. For his return, I gave him kit bags full of grub. "Take them back to my family at Nijverdal." And he did just that, and they were happy.

"We had no professionalism, but we were adventurers. We were go-getters. We were voyageurs. We were full of courage. I lift my hat to the guts of the Canadian soldier."

CHARLES FORBES

CHARLES FORBES

I was born down in the Gaspé at a small town called Matane. Ever since I was a kid, I wanted to be a soldier. I played with soldiers, airplanes, and what not. Deep down in my mind, I had already decided my vocation was soldiering. My father was of Scottish ancestry. In fact, his ancestor was on the Plains of Abraham with the 78th Fraser Highlanders. But then all these Scots married French-Canadian girls, so I hardly spoke a word of English. When I went to Royal Military School (RMC) in Kingston, it was not that easy. One of the cadets said to me when I arrived, "You're a frog." And I said, "No, my name is Forbes." I insisted on that, and we had a few arguments. They were going to close the college in 1942, so a buddy and I decided to enlist right away. I started in artillery, but that wasn't hot enough for me, so I transferred to infantry.

I was sent overseas in December 1943. I was a lieutenant, but I was General List. I wanted to get into the 1st Canadian Paratroops. I was sick and tired of not belonging to a fighting unit. But my colonel told me, "Paratroopers are a bunch of crazy guys. They're going to come down

Lt. Col. Charles Forbes, Master Warrant Officer of the 2nd Canadian Infantry Division, in Belgium, September 1944.

Forbes is at the head of his group as they advance inland through Normandy, 1944. This photograph clearly shows the destructive nature of the battle for control of France.

from the skies like ducks and crows, and they're going to be shot to death." He was a veteran of the First World War, you see. "My boy, the winning battles during this war will be fought on the ground, not on high-tension wires. I will send you to a good unit." The next day I was with the Regiment Maisonneuve. When the CO saw me, he said I had three strikes against me. "First, you were born in the godforsaken Gaspé, not in Montreal. Second, you have an English name. Third, you have been to RMC." That was my introduction. The language of the regiment was French, except when we had to speak to other regiments on the wireless in English with our funny accents.

We headed for Normandy July 6 and were committed to action July 18 for the final liberation of the city of Caen. That was after the horrible bombing in which we killed more than seven thousand French people there. It was not a gift, I'll tell you. My first experience in battle was terrible. I was commanding No. 18 Platoon in Delta Company. The major didn't understand that DP on the map meant Datum Point, where the artillery was to be lined up, and not the infantry's Departure Point. I told him that the infantry starting point is called Start Line, which was not shown on the map. He got pissed off and said, "Are you scared?" And I said, "Yes, sir. I'm scared because you are going to wind up in your own artillery barrage." He told me to take the reserve battalion and I pulled my men back a hundred yards. H-hour came and the barrage began. The Germans saw our own barrage and put another one on top of us. I saved my platoon, but when the operation was over, the major was killed, and there were only forty-two men left in the company from one hundred and twenty.

My first experience confirmed what I thought since I had arrived in England, and this is not because I am sour about it at all. I am not sour a damn bit. But 80 per cent of the officers, from commanding officers to divisional commanders, were ignoramuses. They had read a hell of a lot of books, but war is not fought in books. War is fought on the ground. I saw many mistakes during that war made by people who really had no clue what they were doing.

Slowly, we moved forward, with casualties beyond imagination. There were days in the battalion when we had as many as twenty-seven dead. Multiply your dead by three and you have your wounded. And the shell shock. You won't believe it. Saint-André-sur-Orne. We had to capture it three times. Twice, the Germans took it back. We were facing the Kurt Meyer division, the 12th SS Panzers. These were the young fanatics – eighteen, nineteen years of age. They were the toughest, fiercest fighters. And they had experienced officers who had fought on the Russian front. It was house-to-house fighting in the village. We finally took it. But moving from one hole to another and walking around dead cows, walking around dead bodies. Seeing people suffer. Wounded soldiers. How can I describe that?

I was a platoon commander, and you are the one in closest contact with the enemy because you have to lead your men. You don't tell them to "go there." You say, "Follow me." That's the way we fought in the Canadian Army. We had no professionalism, but we were adventurers. We were go-getters. We were voyageurs. We were full of courage. I lift my hat to the guts of the Canadian soldier. A German officer said once, "I know why the Canadian soldiers fight so well. It is because their officers fight with them." By the end of October, we were tired. Really beat. We had been in battle in France, northern France, Belgium, and Holland. No rest since July.

Walcheren Island was the final battle for the liberation of Antwerp. The city had been freed, but no ships had access to the harbour. That was vital to us because the whole Canadian Army was being supplied by Cherbourg, four hundred kilometres away. Our artillery was reduced to firing about six shells per day per gun. You don't go to war with that. The harbour entrance was controlled by eight-inch, ten-inch, twelve-inch German guns buried in concrete casements on Walcheren Island. On October 31, the weather was very bad. It was freezing. It was raining. It was a combined operation, with British commandos. And the Black Watch was ordered to walk across the causeway and capture the dikes on the banks of the island. The causeway was a thousand yards long, and a sixty-foot-wide target with water on each side. The Black Watch had a hell of a time. They went in with no preparation. The brigade major, George Hees, who became minister of Veterans Affairs, was a glorious man, but the operation was in daylight and utterly ridiculous. Once they were five hundred yards across the causeway, the Germans put a terrific bombardment on and they had to be pulled back.

Then the brigadier committed what I call a major mistake in tactics. Reinforced failure. If a one-inch cork doesn't fit in a bottle, don't try again with a one-inch cork. But he tried to cross the causeway again, this time with the Calgary Highlanders, a fantastic battalion. They made it across to the dikes, but the Germans threw in another murderous counterattack and the Calgarys suffered heavy casualties. They pulled back all the way to the centre of the causeway where there was a big crater.

Courtesy Charles Forbes

A detail from an oil painting by Forbes portraying the battle of
Walcheren in Holland, November 2, 1944.

That night, my Maisonneuve Regiment had been ordered on leave to
the city of Liere. This would be our first rest since Normandy, so we were
all anxious to go. We were shaving, cleaning up. We knew the Calgarys
would make it. But soon I could hear the guns and I knew something was
wrong. When the CO wanted to see me, my hat turned green. He told me,
"Charley, we're attacking over the causeway, through the Calgarys position, to capture the right- and left-hand dikes. You're going to be leading
the attack with your platoon. You go at four o'clock tomorrow morning."

At four o'clock, we were standing by, and the artillery bombardment
began. A huge bombardment. And away we went. I had my machine-gun
guys on each side. The Arsenault brothers from New Brunswick. I told
them, "If you see anything move, just fire and keep firing until we reach

the other side." Just as we were starting to go, I saw some troops moving toward us. We couldn't identify them clearly, so the Arsenault brothers started to fire. Suddenly, in the flash of an explosion, I saw the steel helmets of the Calgarys. We were shooting our own troops down! I had to jump on their backs to stop them. It was a very, very bad start. It more or less broke our spirit and our momentum. We had to regroup. But we did make it to the island.

When we got there, an anti-tank gun was firing. So the boys jumped on the two gunners. They surrendered. Guy Demarie was following me with No. 17 Platoon. I told him, "Let's go." But we couldn't see. The artillery had stopped firing. There was no longer any light. We were on the island and all we could see was water. I figured we still had to get to the two dikes. So we kept on running. His platoon on the left-hand side, mine on the right. There was no opposition. We didn't see a single German soldier. We ran and ran until we came to an overpass. We suddenly realized that in the excitement, we had bypassed our objectives and gone five hundred yards inside the island. Jesus. We decided to hold it there, and wait for the British to come.

Six o'clock passed. Seven o'clock. We didn't see any Brits. We waited and waited, hanging on, ladderlike, to the bank of the dike. Then I saw movement in the fog and the rain. A column of troops was coming toward us along the bank. I yelled to my boys, "Be careful, now. I think it's the Brits. Don't fire. Let's go and meet them." I'm about to pull myself out of the water, and I recognized the German helmet. Lord and God! So I got back into my hole, holding my pistol in one hand, and I waited for the Germans to come. I yelled, "When I open fire, fire!" We fired on them at close range. I hit the first one in the shoulder with my pistol. He fell in the water. Then we emptied a couple of mags of Bren guns and rifle fire. There was a moment of quiet, and fifty to sixty German troops were then withdrawing along the bank. But we were right in the middle of a bees' nest. What could we do? We were all lying in water, as close to the bank as we could, to protect ourselves. We tried to pull the man I had shot out of the water as the tide was going up. But I pulled on the arm that had been dislocated, where he was bleeding badly. He yelled, so I had to leave him there. I was exposed. The Germans started to creep toward our position. Sniping at us. By then, it was four o'clock in the afternoon. At last we were given orders to withdraw and we made it back to the start of the causeway.

I asked for a smokescreen and started to run back across the causeway toward to the mainland. We had a thousand yards to go. As we were running, one of the German heavy guns was firing at the causeway. A shell hit one of my soldiers, Talbot. Shrapnel in the spine. I said, "Don't move. I'll drag you into a hole." We took cover and I looked at his wound. There seemed to be a bit of steel caught between two vertebrae. I decided to pull it out right there, and he felt better.

I stayed with Talbot until eleven o'clock at night. When we finally made it back to our lines, they put Talbot in an ambulance and I looked around for any soldiers from our battalion. There wasn't a goddamned soul to be seen. The ambulance driver told me, "Your battalion has gone to Belgium for a rest. Enjoy yourself, buster." I got so sour and sad inside. I started to shake. I was wet. I was frozen. I was hungry. And particularly, I was hurt inside. I thought at least someone could have been left behind when they went on leave. There were some Dutch Resistance there and I said, "I'm completely finished. I'm out. I'm going nuts." I could hear the sound of machine-gun bullets flying through my head. They took me to a Dutch house, and the girls made some hot-water bottles and they laid me on a bed and I stayed there for a couple of days. They looked after me as if I was a twenty-carat diamond. I regained some of my energy. In the meantime, my mother received a telegram that I'd been reported missing. Eventually, she got another wire saying they had found me. Or, that I had found myself.

I finally hooked up with my battalion in Liere, but five days later, on the way back to cross the Maas River, a German artillery shell killed my driver and wounded my right eye quite deeply. The medics picked me up and put me in a barber's chair. They put a piece of wood in my teeth and a corporal sewed my eye up cold. No injections whatsoever. He did a rough job. He told me it would have to be redone, "but I'm going to do it so you don't get infected." They fixed it up with plastic surgery back in England.

Lt. Col. Charles Forbes made a career with the armed forces and fought
with the Royal 22nd Regiment, 2nd Battalion, in the Korean War.

In 1945, the corps commander approved that I be the recipient of the
highest Dutch decoration, which is their equivalent of the Victoria Cross.
Then the war ended, and that was that.

I have asked myself many times how I did it. Six months under terrible stress, enduring war with all its ugliness. I have killed three times. It is
terrible to kill to save your skin. It's shoot or get shot. Like what happened

on Walcheren Island with the man I shot in the shoulder. And when Fortie, one of my men, was killed and left behind. All these things. You get to be a zombie. One day after the other. One step at a time. The left foot goes down. The right foot replaces it. That's the way an operation goes. You do your best, but you wear down. One of my corporals broke down in Brussels. He had come with me all the way from Caen. He was dressed like a funeral director: top hat and a black coattail. He was arrested by a British MP. My case was the same after I was hit in the eye. I was shaking all over. I had lost my place. You have no idea what it's like, when you're lying on the frozen ground, scratches on your hands that are full of puss, and you are trying to grab a bit of sleep, and you start to urinate. You're like a spring on a clock that goes and goes, and as long as there's some energy left, it keeps marking the time.

"We went over on the *Queen Elizabeth*.
There were more than fifteen thousand
troops and one kid kept saying,
'There's more people on this ship
than in my hometown.'"

ESTELLE TRITT-ASPLER

ESTELLE TRITT-ASPLER

I was born April 26, 1919, in Montreal. I went into nurse training at Montreal General Hospital in 1938. I was good at medical and surgical care, and I liked obstetrics. In those days, we kept new mothers in bed for nine days. On the tenth day, they could swing their legs. On the eleventh day, they could sit in a chair. How things have changed! Now, they're out before they're in.

I graduated in 1941, and went to work at the Jewish General. I was there for a year. Twelve hours on, twelve hours off. My brother, Jackie, was in the air force by then, and I decided to join the army. That's where they needed nurses. There was work to be done. Unfortunately, Jackie was killed shortly after I joined up. They asked me whether I wanted to be released. I said, "No thanks. When do I go over?" I was sent to a military hospital in Kingston, Ontario, where I got my basic training. We learned to march and how to salute, and how you do everything. Then we had embarkation and my family came down to see us off. My mother said, "Oh, there are an awful lot of girls here." And I said, "Oh yes, Mom. We're

Lt. Nursing Sr. Estelle Tritt-Aspler of the 18th Canadian General Hospital in dress uniform, 1944.

THE MONTREAL DAILY STAR, MONDAY, AUGUST 2, 1943

Quebec Nurses in Britain

—Canadian Army Photo.

Three Quebec Nursing Sisters have arrived overseas with a General Hospital, R.C.A.M.C., of Cobourg, Ontario. They are, as pictured above, left to right, Nursing Sisters Estelle Tritt, of Montreal; Ruth Gaw, of Huntingdon; Winnona Lindsay, Notre Dame du Sacre Coeur.

Tritt-Aspler (far left) and two other nurses arrive in Britain for the war effort, as covered by the Montreal *Daily Star* on August 2, 1943.

opening a new hospital in Cobourg, Ontario." That's what I told her. But somewhere along the line, a picture was taken of me and two other girls sitting on a bench in Truro, Nova Scotia, and after we were overseas, it was in the papers. I got a letter from my mother, "It's nice to know where you are by reading the papers." I apologized, but I didn't want to tell her I was going overseas.

We went over on the *Queen Elizabeth*. There were twelve of us in a cubbyhole with triple-decker bunks. No two people could stand at one time. There were more than fifteen thousand troops and one kid kept saying, "There's more people on this ship than in my hometown." This was 1943, and we were excited. We landed in England and went to Bramshott, where we had an eight-hundred-bed hospital. There was one section for bad boys. Those with VD or ones who had gone AWOL and had different medical problems. I wasn't on that ward, thank goodness. A Norwegian air-force boy, who was courting one of our girls, taught me how to ride a bicycle. Then I went to No. 8 Canadian General, which was in Farnborough. We had some fellows there who had been at Dieppe, and we had other

Tritt-Aspler and others from No. 8 Canadian General Hospital (CGH)
scrounging wood for fireplaces in 1944.

injuries. Hitler's secret weapon was the motorcycle, because we had a lot
of fellows there who got hurt that way, riding motorcycles. For a period,
we had a lowland Scottish division that had come in from the Middle East.
They were all down with malaria. Some of them were quite sick, but as
soon as they were up and about, they got into fights and were brought
back. Some of those fellows were brought back with four or five MPs, having beaten up all the MPs. It was quite a time.

Before D-Day, we were put into isolation, because we were only going
to treat those who had been briefed about it. I lived in a house down the
road from the hospital and there were guards walking up and down, making sure we didn't contact anyone. We couldn't go bicycling anywhere.
This began about six weeks before D-Day. The night before D-Day and
early morning, we could hear the planes going over and over all the time.
And we knew D-Day had started. Then we started to get patients. People
would be treated on the beaches. They would be returned to England to a

hospital and, within a few hours, shipped to another hospital. I remember the boys coming in. We didn't look at them as patients. We looked at them as kids who had injuries. I hope they appreciated me.

A few weeks later, Matron Harvey announced that three nurses were needed to go to France. So I did what the boys told me never to do. I put my hand up. I volunteered. I just felt like doing it. I wanted to be closer to the troops. We had to wear battledress, khaki shirts. It felt funny. I was very heavy at the time, and to find a size that would fit me, oh dear. We arrived in France on Bastille Day, July 14. Arromaches. It was an amazing sight to see. We were boarded onto trucks and went into the countryside singing the first two lines of "La Marseillaise."

We landed on the Bayeux road and there were hospitals on every side. Our fellows set up tents for the patients and tents for us. It was my first time camping. We had a folding cot, a washstand on a tripod, things like that. Two to a tent. Our rations were British. M and V. Meat and vegetables. And SPAM. I think it was from South America. It wasn't very good. But there was a farmhouse nearby, where they had sour cream, and Dorothy Callback and I went there. Everybody said we were going to be sick. And I said, "No. I was brought up on sour cream."

We started to get German POWs. As a matter of fact, I spoke a little Yiddish, and certain words are similar to German. I was working with one of the doctors, and could ask a patient if he was married or something basic. And the doctor said afterwards, "I didn't know you could speak German." I said, "I don't. I speak a bit of Yiddish." And he said, "My God, does he know?" A friend of mine had gone to the Jewish People's School in Montreal and knew Yiddish very well. One of the young German soldiers asked her, "How come you understand me, and the others don't?" And she said, "I'm Jewish, and I know Yiddish." He looked at her and said, "Oh. The Jews are people?"

I had a lad in with a bad case of tonsillitis, who joined the army after D-Day. Now how much basic training did he have? Zero. People didn't understand that after Dieppe and Italy, Canada sent kids, and there was no way they were well trained. We also had to treat SIWs. Self-inflicted wounds. There were about ten or fifteen of them. There was one lad who

6			7	
ARTICLE	QUANTITY		ARTICLE	QUANTITY
Cover, mess tin..........			Veil, face, camouflage............	
Frogs, web, bayonet......			Yoke.....	
Haversack............			*Line Not Whipcords*	
Helmet, steel........			*Notes on War Clothes*	
Net camouflage helmet....			Capes, A/G. ...	
Packs.........			Respirators, A/G, complete with haversack.....	
Pockets Compass......			Outfits, A/D....	
Pouches, amm, pistol......			Ointment, A/G....	2
Pouches, basic.....			Eyeshields, A/G, pk of 6....	
Pouches, utility { Front / Rear.....			Detectors, Individual, prs....	2
Slings, rifle, web........			Wallet, A/G... *Cotton Wasting*	
Straps, shoulder, haversack { left / right...			Blanket....	
Straps, web, supporting........			*FA for Fighting Men*	
Tins, mess, TP.......			Mug, drinking....	
Initials of Soldier........			Sheet, ground.....	
Initials of QM or Rep...			Initials of Soldier....	
			Initials of QM or Rep....	

A page from Tritt-Aspler's clothing and equipment statement,
tracking the various items that she had been issued, 1944.

doctors said could serve as a cook or a driver but not on the front lines.
And they put him on the front line. He lasted for some time and then shot
himself in the leg or something. The fellows with SIW were never charged.
No one had time. There was no attempt to do psychological work with
them. They were moved to a hospital nearer to the front. It was almost like
they had leprosy. God knows what happened to them in the end.

I was transferred to No. 6 Canadian General, a two-hundred-bed hospital in Belgium. Our dentist went to his senior officer and said, "I'm fill-
ing the teeth of the English, the French, the Dutch, the Polish. Where are
all the Canadians?" The reply was, "Who the hell do you think are in the
Canadian Army now?" We did not have enough reinforcements. I remember a funny incident there. They brought in a young American boy who'd
been injured by a flying bomb. When he came to, he was hooked up to an

IV, blood transfusion, tubing every which way. He opened his eyes, looked around, and said, "I thought they told me there was a rubber shortage."

In Belgium and when we went up to Holland, I started searching for other Jewish people. There just seemed to be no Jews around. I found some who had been hidden, some who had served in the underground. But the Jewish population was just destroyed. What do you say when you meet someone who was taken for forced labour and managed to escape and went back home to find his wife and child had been deported? What do you say to a woman who says her daughter was deported? There were things like that. We didn't know the full extent. We knew people had been deported, but we didn't quite know what had happened to them. Some survived because people took them in. It is amazing what some people did. A lot of them paid with their lives. One woman showed me a picture of a child holding someone's hand. You couldn't see whose hand she was holding. You couldn't tell what street they were on. You couldn't tell anything. But this was the only proof she had that her child was okay.

When I was posted to Holland, near 's-Hertogenbosch, which was known for its chocolate, another Jewish nursing sister and I attended a Seder together. We had met some people there and they invited us. There were about ten or twelve of us, and for some of them, it was their first Seder in a long time. They were traumatized and in rough shape. There were a lot of tears and emotion. It was a very unusual evening. The family that gave the Seder had two teenaged children who refused to speak German. There was another lad there, and he was wondering what happened to his parents. Should he stay and look for them, or join the Dutch Army? There was also a rabbi from Germany who looked as if he'd had TB. He was underground during the war, in the Resistance. It was the only Seder I attended until I returned to Canada. I always had my Jewish faith. I didn't always observe it, but I tried to observe it more after this. Wherever I went, I tried to find Jewish people.

We went up to Gronigen. They had a synagogue. I met a young woman there. She had a four-year-old boy who had been placed with people for his own safety and hers. Now, he clung to her all the time, because he was scared that he would be placed again. Whenever he saw a stranger,

Tritt-Aspler (far left) on leave in France with fellow army
hospital personnel in the spring of 1945.

he ran like hell. She had given birth to a baby in a Dutch nursing home.
They didn't give her anaesthetic for fear that she might blurt out something that would indicate she was Jewish. I remember two other Jewish
women weeping. Their daughters had been taken. God knows where they
were. One of them said she and her daughter had been taken somewhere.
Her daughter was put on a train, and a German officer told her, "Oh, you
go home." He thought she was too old. She would die anyway.

At home people would hear that I was overseas, and they would ask
my mother to wire me. "Oh, can you please try and find so-and-so." There
was a child living with people in California who kept crying about her
sister and her parents. I found out that her sister was in unoccupied
France and seemed to be okay, but the parents had been deported. A little
later I went to Amsterdam and asked the Sally Ann to look into it. Just as I

was leaving, I got a phone call that the girl's mother was in some hostel there. So my ambulance driver stopped off at this place and I went in to see the mother. When she came in, I couldn't help thinking, There, but for the grace of God, goes my mother. The father was dead. Then I got another cable. Some boy was in one camp and his mother in another. Try to find them. I wrote to the Search Bureau and they wrote back that the two had been reunited. So some stories didn't turn out too badly.

For a brief time, we were in Germany, not far from the Holland border. We took over what had been a big nursing home. The people who had owned it came back and were quite indignant that we had taken it over. They forgot about everything that the Germans took. There was no fraternizing in Germany. We didn't like the Germans and had very little contact with them. We were not happy there. We didn't have much room, but we did get two young Polish girls who had been taken from Poland and used by the German soldiers. We had to send them to a Dutch hospital, where they died a few days later. Cause of death: TB, VD. You name it, they had it. Poor kids.

The day the war ended, there wasn't a big celebration. There was only one feeling. Relief. We just sat around and said, "Thank God." I enjoyed the companionship of the people I worked with. I enjoyed working with the boys and helping them. I made friends that I maintained for many years. There was triage for the wounded, so by the time we got them, it wasn't exactly hell for us. It wasn't good, but it wasn't hell. It was just a question of getting through.

Allied troops talking a time out from battle, France, 1944.

ACKNOWLEDGEMENTS

This book is a result of the combined efforts of a remarkable group of individuals and organizations. First and foremost, I'd like to thank Rod Mickleburgh, who so expertly crafted the participating veterans' oral testimonial into the moving vignettes that constitute this collection. Vital to this project from its outset also has been the enthusiastic support of McClelland & Stewart and the leadership provided by our editors, Dinah Forbes and Elizabeth Kribs. The hard work and dedication of Dominion Institute staff members Jennifer Jeynes-Holmes and David Harkness was essential in bringing together the vast collection of veterans' personal artifacts and images that complement each testimonial.

Rare Courage is an extension of the Dominion Institute's Memory Project. We salute the following organizations for their exceptional support of our ongoing work with veterans: Veterans Affairs Canada, the Department of Canadian Heritage, the Government of Ontario, the Royal Canadian Legion, Home Hardware Stores Limited, and the *Globe and Mail*.

If you are a veteran or know a veteran who would like to volunteer with the Dominion Institute and share his or her war experiences with young people, please contact us at staff@dominion.ca or call us toll-free at 1-866-701-1867.

All proceeds generated by the sale of this book will be used by the Dominion Institute to help veterans visit with youth across Canada.

GLOSSARY

GENERAL TERMS

Baptism of fire. Soldiers' expression for first experience of combat.

Batman. A soldier assigned as a personal assistant to any commissioned officer.

Blighty. Slang for England. Used by troops serving abroad.

CANLOAN. A program that permitted the lending of surplus Canadian officers to the British Army. Under this scheme, 673 Canadian officers volunteered to serve in British Army units, from early 1944 to the end of the war.

Flick turn. This manoeuvre was used by fighter pilots to effect a 180-degree turn quickly. It is a slow-speed, high-rate turn that uses the pull of gravity to quicken the rate of turn by going from a "nose-high" to a "nose-low" turn reversal.

Honey-bucket duty. Latrine cleaning duty.

Looking down moon. Having the moon at your back so that the moonlight illuminates or silhouettes whatever is in front of you.

Jerry. Second World War soldiers' slang for Germans.

Mae West. A floatation vest/life preserver. It was named after the 1930s film star because its large inflatable portions rested directly over the wearer's chest.

Non-commissioned officers (NCOS). Military personnel from the rank of corporal to warrant officer first class, who, although they have significant authority and responsibility, do not hold a King or Queen's commission.

Pillbox. A small concrete defensive structure for a machine gun or an anti-tank weapon.

Sally Ann. Slang term for the Salvation Army, which often provided amenities and soldiers' comforts to troops serving overseas.

Wolf pack. The term given to the German tactic of having as many U-boats as possible converge on an Allied sea convoy in order to sink the most tonnage.

PEOPLE/BATTLES/EVENTS

Black Watch. The Black Watch (Royal Highland Regiment) of Canada. An infantry battalion that served in the 5th Brigade of the 2nd Canadian Infantry Division during the Second World War.

Bomber Harris. Air Marshall Arthur "Bomber" Harris remains one of the most controversial military commanders of the Second World War. He was head of Bomber Command during the Allies' massive air campaign against Nazi Germany between 1942 and 1945. Harris was a believer that the bombing of civilian targets, and as a result civilians, would shorten the Second World War.

Camp Borden (Base Borden). A large military training establishment in southern Ontario, northwest of Toronto. It covers an area of 20,000 acres (8,094 hectares) and also includes an armoured-vehicle range at Meaford, to the northwest. Camp Borden was used during the Second World War as a training/deployment facility.

Camp Lee. Camp Lee, Virginia, was designated the Quartermaster Replacement Training Center in February 1941. By the end of the Second World War, approximately three hundred thousand enlisted soldiers received basic and branch training at Camp Lee, and an additional fifty thousand soldiers went through Officer Candidate School there.

El Alamein (Battle of). A North African battle between Gen. Sir Bernard Law Montgomery's British Eighth Army and German Field Marshal Erwin Rommel's Italo-German Army, October 23–November 5, 1942. A great victory for the Allies, the battle of El Alamein initiated Rommel's withdrawal from Egypt.

D-Day. This term usually refers to the commencement of Operation OVERLORD, the Allied invasion of Normandy, June 6, 1944. In more generic terms, "d-day" simply refers to the unnamed day on which a particular operation is to commence.

Field Marshal the Viscount Montgomery of Alamein. British General of the Second World War. He commanded the British Eighth Army in North Africa, Sicily, and Italy (August 1942–January 1944), after which he went on to command the Twenty-first Army Group (January 1944–August 1945). The 1st Canadian Infantry Division and the 1st Canadian Armoured Brigade fought under Montgomery's Eighth Army in Sicily and Italy and the 1st Canadian

Army served with the Twenty-first Army Group during the war in northwest Europe.

Field Marshal Erwin Rommel. Nicknamed the "Desert Fox," Rommel earned a reputation as a masterful tactician and strategist in North Africa. After his evacuation from Tunisia, he went on to command Army Group B in northern France, where he was responsible for the German defence of Normandy against the Allies.

The Great Escape. The escape of seventy-six Allied prisoners of war from Stalag Luft III on the night of March 24–25, 1944. Despite their initial success, all but three of the escapees were recaptured within a few days and more than fifty of them were executed by German authorities. A 1963 Hollywood film of the same name retold the story.

Juno Beach. The beach that the 3rd Canadian Infantry Division assaulted on D-Day. The beach itself was divided into smaller beaches – "Nan" Beach in the east and "Mike" Beach in the west. "Nan" Beach, the larger of the two, was subdivided further from east to west into sectors Red, White, and Green. "Mike" Beach had only two sectors, Red and Green.

Operation DYNAMO. The operation during which 848 British, Dutch, French, and Belgian ships evacuated more than 338,000 British and Allied troops from Dunkirk, May 26–June 3, 1940.

WEAPONS

Ack-ack gun. Slang term for any anti-aircraft gun.

Bofors gun. A 40 mm light anti-aircraft gun that could engage targets effectively to a height of 12,500 feet.

Bren gun. British light machine gun, which fired .303 ammunition from a curved thirty-round magazine.

Buzz bombs. Name given to the German V-1 flying bomb because of the buzzing sound of its engine. Often referred to as the first cruise missile, this weapon had a range of 330 kilometres and was used against targets in southeastern England and Belgium between June 1944 and March 1945.

Nebelwurfer. A German six-barrelled rocket launcher, also known as the Moaning Minnie.

Pom-pom gun. An anti-aircraft gun, usually a one-pounder or a two-pounder, named for the sound the weapon made when firing.

Sten gun. A British submachine gun.

Tommy gun. A Thompson submachine gun.

Tracers. Bullets containing a chemical composition that burns brightly as the projectile travels through the air, giving the illusion of a bright streak between the firer and the target.

Vickers machine gun. A British machine gun that weighed more than forty pounds and fired .303 rounds at a rate of 450 rounds per minute.

Weasel. A tracked vehicle designed for use in the snow.

SHIPS/PLANES

Bismarck. A German battleship launched in 1940. The *Bismarck* menaced Allied shipping until it was finally sunk May 27, 1941.

Dornier Do 217. German four-seat bomber, which also had a three-seat night-fighter variant.

Focke-Wulf 190. A single-seat German fighter and attack aircraft in service from 1941 to 1945. An exceptional aircraft, it was smaller than the British Spitfire, which it could outmanoeuvre, and had four 20 mm cannons as well as two machine guns for armament.

HMS *Hood.* One of the largest battleships of the Second World War, the British HMS *Hood* was sunk by the German battleship *Bismarck* May 24, 1941.

Junkers 88 (Ju 88). A versatile German bomber, capable of speeds up to 480 kilometres per hour. In service from 1939 to 1945, the Ju 88, despite its speed as a bomber, was vulnerable to the Spitfire and Hurricane fighters of the RAF during the Battle of Britain.

Lancaster bomber. British heavy bomber. Capable of carrying a fourteen-thousand-pound bomb load, the seven-seat Lancaster was the workhorse of the bomber offensive against Germany.

Landing Craft Assault (LCA). A lightly armoured landing craft capable of carrying up to thirty-six troops. These craft were designed for the first wave of an amphibious assault.

Landing Craft Control (LCC). A lead-in navigational craft for landing boats. The LCC had a steel hull and collapsible antennae and radar and was used to mark the line of departure, for traffic control, and for preliminary hydrographic surveys.

Landing Craft Infantry (LCI). A flat-bottomed landing craft capable of carrying two hundred troops. These craft were only used for second and subsequent waves of amphibious assault, after the main beach defences had been cleared.

Landing Craft Tank (LCT). A landing craft designed to bring tanks ashore in second and subsequent waves of amphibious assault. Each LCT could carry four tanks.

Liberty boats. Boats that ferried sailors to and from shore, usually for the purpose of leave.

Messerschmitt 109. German single-seat fighter in service from 1937 to 1945. Although the Messerschmitt 109 outclassed the British Spitfire at the beginning of the war, by 1945 improved Allied fighters, including the Spitfire, were able to outperform it.

Spitfire. British single-seat fighter that first proved itself during the Battle of Britain. The main aircraft of Fighter Command, more than twenty thousand Spitfires of many different models were produced for the Royal Air Force.

Whirlwind. British single-seat, twin-engine fighter in service from 1940 to 1943. Not as manoeuvrable at higher altitudes as the Spitfire, the Whirlwind was better suited for bomber escorts or in low-level raids.